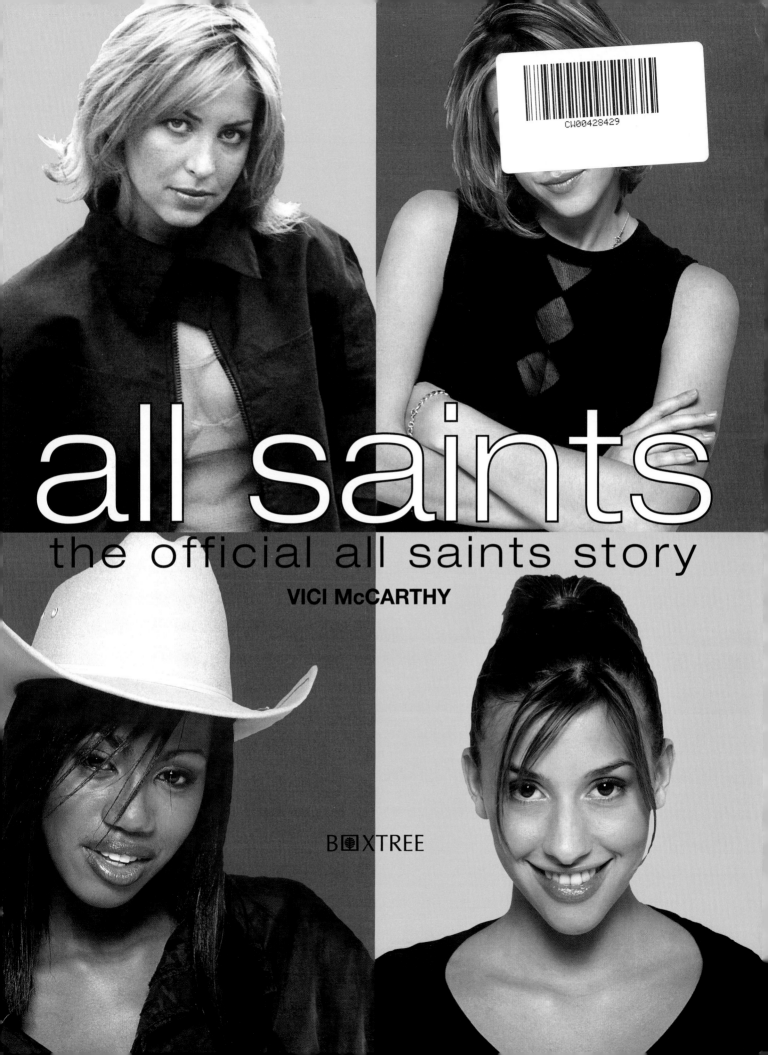

# all saints

## the official all saints story

**VICI McCARTHY**

B☒XTREE

First published in 1998 by Boxtree, an imprint of Macmillan Publishers Ltd,
25 Eccleston Place, London, SW1W 9NF and Basingstoke

Associated companies throughout the world

ISBN 0 7522 1334 2

9 8 7 6 5 4 3 2 1

A CIP catalogue record for this book is available from the British Library

Design and reproduction by Blackjacks, London
Printed by Bath Press

**Photographs:** All Action: 2, 6 (left), 10, 18, 19, 22 (left), 27 (bottom left & right), 30 (left), 33, 34, 35, 38, 40, 44, 47 (top and bottom), 48 (bottom), 50, 53, 54, 55, 56, 58-9, 64, 67, 68. Redferns: 8, 11 (right), 14 (middle left), 26, 27 (top left), 32 (bottom), 42, 44, 45, 51, 52, 57, 62-3. Zed Nelson: 13, 14 (top and bottom left), 20 (right), 21 (bottom), 29 (middle), 36 (left), 49 (bottom), 60, 61, 69, 70, 71. News Team: 70 (top).
Childhood photographs: All Saints. All other photographs: Ray Burmiston.

# AUTHOR'S NOTE

The first time I met All Saints I felt like I'd been ripped straight from the plot of *Planes, Trains and Automobiles*.

I was supposed to have met the girls at a video set, in London's Old Street, at 9 a.m. The cab had been booked for 7.30. At 7.40 it was 'just around the corner' and it stayed 'just around the corner' for another forty-five minutes.

At 9 a.m., stuck in traffic on the Archway Road, I jumped out and caught a tube, arriving, bewildered, in east London at 9.45. I was lost, couldn't find my bearings and the heavens opened to torrential rain.

I was done for.

I arrived, eventually, at the studio over an hour late, soaked to the skin, hair dripping onto the floor, mascara running down my cheeks, convinced that I'd lost my interview, and walked slap bang into Melanie Blatt, who grinned when she saw the state I was in.

'Don't wooooorrrry!' she said. 'It's not a proooblem!'

'I didn't even know you were late!' said Shaznay.

And while Nic made me a cup of tea, and tour manager Johnny Buckland found me a towel to dry my hair, the girls joked about, making sarnies and gossiping, giving me a good half hour to calm down before helping me with the interviews.

In ten years of interviewing celebrities I'd never experienced such relief! Welcome to the All Saints camp.

While researching this book I've talked to masses of people who've worked with, or come into contact with, All Saints, and the one phrase that keeps cropping up to describe them is 'nice girls'.

And they are.

All Saints are four girls who have worked hard to get where they are. They've come across wheelers and dealers, schemers and rip-off merchants, but through it all they've remained pleasant solid girls who love life and give everyone a chance. There's not a lot of that goes down in the music industry!

Thanks, then, to Shaznay, Nic, Nat and Mel for their honest interviews (especially Mel for her advice on making the words big so people will want to read them!) and thanks also to the following:

Mel and Eugene at London Records, Jenny Olivier for the whiskeys, all at John Benson Music Management, Billy Molloy (Down with dat sorta ting. Careful now) and all at *Sky* magazine. Information in this book has also been taken from interviews with *Smash Hits*, *Vox*, *FHM*, *Loaded*, *Top Of The Pops* magazine, *Bliss*, *The Face*, *The NME*, *Melody Maker* and *Mizz*.

Additional interview material by the lovely Sian Pattenden.

Credit has been given where it's due! With thanks.

Vici McCarthy

# INTRODUCTION

Tucked in behind the Westway, near London's Ladbroke Grove, is All Saints Road — a small street, just a few blocks long, of tall terraced, painted buildings.

It's a trendy address, home of the famous W11 restaurant The Sugar Club, and dotted with various upholstery and music shops. But hidden inconspicuously among its edifices there was once a recording studio, Metamorphosis: the birthplace of All Saints.

For two years, Shaznay Lewis and Melanie Blatt pretty much called the studio 'home'. For the pair of them, their hang-out was a university. Shaznay sang back-up vocals, Mel studied other musicians at work, and together the duo tried to craft together songs and demos in pursuit of their one goal: they wanted to make music. Professionally.

More than half a decade later, Mel and Shaznay's band, All Saints, is something like a phenomenon. Newspapers, music magazines and music industry insiders are stunned by the girls' achievements: within months of releasing their debut London Records single, the girls, together with Nicole and Natalie Appleton, made a credible mark on the world music scene, raking in number-one singles, platinum-selling records and music awards.

Their talent, foresight and refusal to compromise have inspired legions of young musicians who have realised that, among the novelty records, hyped-up artists and marketing ploys of the music industry, there is still room for people dedicated to producing good music. All Saints have taken some of the emphasis off 'industry' and shifted it onto 'music'. They're definitely one of the more dynamic success stories of the late 90s!

The All Saints story isn't a simple one, of course. They have suffered false starts, upsets and set-backs. Ever since their teenage days at the studio, the girls have had to tear down obstacle after obstacle to get to their present position, overcoming the early-90s boy-band phenomenon, then girl-band mania (not to mention preconceptions of them based on their appearance) to get to a situation where they could be fully in charge of their own destiny. Theirs really is a case of reaping what they've sown.

Shaznay Lewis, Melanie Blatt, Nicole and Natalie Appleton have had to fight to get their success, but now they've got it, they're enjoying it — and hundreds of thousands of record-buying punters are doing it alongside them! This book intends to show how, with determination, the right intentions and self-belief, it is possible to overcome pretty much anything to achieve your dreams. And, as Shaznay will explain later, all it takes is a bit of nous, honesty, and sticking to your guns...

MELANIE

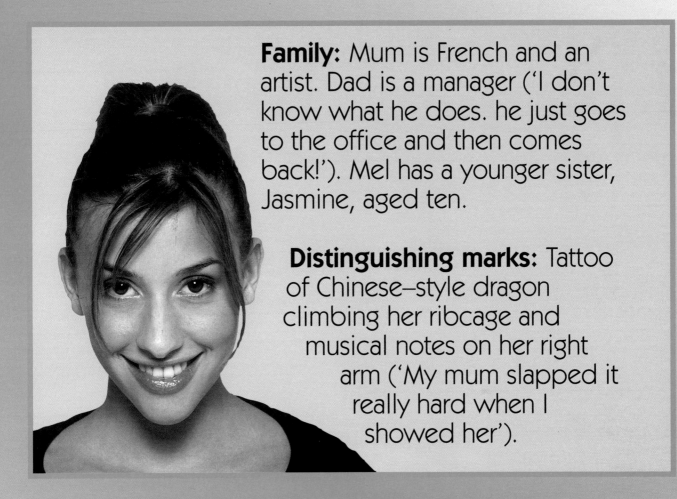

**Family:** Mum is French and an artist. Dad is a manager ('I don't know what he does. he just goes to the office and then comes back!'). Mel has a younger sister, Jasmine, aged ten.

**Distinguishing marks:** Tattoo of Chinese–style dragon climbing her ribcage and musical notes on her right arm ('My mum slapped it really hard when I showed her').

'I was born in London on 25 March 1975, at University College hospital near Euston. I've lived all over London during my life. My parents, Helen and David, moved every couple of years. They often moved to a nicer place when they got a bit more money. My parents were hippies so they were into The Rolling Stones, Led Zeppelin, Rory Gallagher, Stackridge, Yes, Status Quo (when they were cool) and Cat Stevens. My dad had the hugest record collection ever, but I got into my own style early on.'

# R BLATT

**M**el Blatt was six years old when she made her first rock festival performance — just Mel, her violin and, for a stage, the roof of her mum and dad's car. Her one-girl show, at Glastonbury Festival, may not have made much of an impact on the punters that day, but for Mel it remained in her mind as her earliest memory.

It makes a good sound bite, doesn't it? — Girl with bohemian parents born into a musical family. But this isn't clever press — no manufactured publicity story. Despite the fact that Mel would probably prefer you to think her singing mentor was Julie *Sound of Music* Andrews ('She was!' she laughs. 'She made me want to start singing!'), probably closer to the truth is that we have her parents to thank for her career. Mel was born into it.

'I grew up with 70s rock,' she explains. 'My mum and dad went through that hippie thing — they actually named me after Melanie [late 60s 'chanteuse'] so that's sort of my heritage. It's probably because of that that I started listening to R&B!'

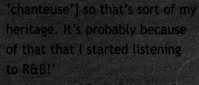

'Mum and Dad always took me to whatever concert I wanted to go to. I'd hear something on the radio and I'd ask, "Can we go?" I was very, very lucky like that. My parents encouraged me loads.'

Not that her parents had much choice in the matter. As a child Mel was probably not that different from her present-day persona — tiny (even today she stands at just 5ft 3in), tough and a bit of an eccentric, but, most of all, totally dedicated to being a singer.

'I think my mum thought of me as being a bit of an eccentric in those days,' she grins. 'I didn't know it until my mum said to me, "When you were a kid everyone thought you were mad!" At that age all my friends wanted to be policemen and doctors, and I wanted to be a singer. Always have.'

Despite the fact that the Blatts moved around a lot when Mel was younger, she didn't have to change schools that much and, fortunately, her first experience of the British education system put her immediately on track towards her goal.

'I went to Fitzjohn's Primary School in Hampstead and there was a really good head teacher called David Joyner,' she remembers. 'The best thing was that they taught music there and the staff were lovely. My favourite subjects were art and singing — I was never pushed towards mathematics really, it never grabbed me (Bohemian parents, you see).

'I remember I played violin and piano, but do I remember anything now? No! I got up to Grade Two piano, actually, and passed Grade One violin. After that I just left it alone. I think that the only reason I played violin was probably that some guy in my class was going to play violin so I thought I'd get in there and play as well.'

Mel made a huge impact at Fitzjohn's, so much so that when the time came for her to leave and head off to senior school, even the staff were aware that she was probably heading for some kind of career in the entertainment industry.

'My mum never said singing wasn't a proper job so I never felt I was trying to do something that wasn't possible,' she explains.

'At school I was known as the showbiz one. When it came to sending me to secondary school the headmaster called up my parents and said, "There's no point in sending her to normal school, she's not normal. Why don't you try stage school?"'

'The first record I bought was Chaka Khan's *I Feel for You* album and then I started buying twelve-inch singles because they were larger and the picture on the sleeve was bigger! I didn't know it was cool.'

Mel was well into the idea in principle, and tried out for the Sylvia Young Theatre School in Marylebone, London. The day she went to do her academic test she cried and ran out of the building 'Because I couldn't get any of the answers. It wasn't that they were hard, it's just that I was so nervous.' Somehow, however, she managed to get accepted, and her 'official' training for a musical career began.

It didn't quite turn out to be as she expected.

'It was terrible. It was just nine-year-olds wearing full make-up, everybody competing against each other for roles. Not healthy, d'ya know what I mean?

'Already I wasn't a competitive person so I wasn't one to say, "I must improve myself to be part of this." I had dark hair, I had bags under my eyes and that wasn't what got you parts in adverts and stuff.They don't like that when you're young! Anyway, I never did that many auditions.

'The one thing I did that I loved was in *Les Misérables*. I was understudy for Corsette and I played Ebony for six months. That was very cool. I had a great time — I was nervous for the first couple of weeks but I soon got into it.

'I loved singing, that was my favourite, but I wasn't given solos because certain girls were favourites and stuff. I never had any of the glory at school. You had to be perfect. It was a lack of confidence I suffered from from then on.'

Mel wasn't into the vibe at all. She did end up in a couple of telly ads — one for Mentadent Gel with Nic and Spice Girl Emma Bunton ('You can't see me,' she grins) and a spaghetti ad ('which I know will come back to haunt me') — but generally, while the other kids ran around auditioning for kids' telly and West End shows, Mel was trying to hang out in recording studios, hoping to pick up backing singing work.

Luckily Mel had a soul-mate to help her through it all — someone who was feeling as lost at the school as she was. Enter Nic Appleton. Within a week of joining Sylvia Young's the pair were inseparable. Mel clocked Nic, Nic clocked Mel, and they've been bezzie mates ever since.

'Nic and I were together, from, like, year dot,' Mel laughs. 'We're partners in crime.

'We can't remember how we met or how it started, but it was an instant bonding and the year we spent together seems like ten years. I dunno. She always makes me laugh. It's the humour, I think, that brought us together. She used to make me wet myself laughing. Still does (usually when I'm not supposed to be, like at a photoshoot!). We were mates like "that". We just couldn't get into the school though.'

Unfortunately, just a year or so after they met, Mel had to hit the pause button on the Blatt-Appleton partnership when a little unforeseen problem became apparent.

Mel got ill.

It turned out that, while she'd been pirouetting and tapping away at school, she'd developed scoliosis — otherwise known as curvature of the spine — so it was looking like the end of her dancing career. If she was lucky.

'It wasn't good,' she explains. 'Here's what happened. Somewhere along the line someone noticed that I had a weird bend in my back, so my mum took me to the doctors. They had a look at it, did all their tests and stuff, and then they said, "You've got this thing called scoliosis."

'My mum was like, "Well, what can we do with it?" and the NHS told us that I could have an operation which had a fifty per cent chance of leaving me paralysed from the neck down. My mother, who's French, said, "Right, that's it. We're out of this country" and we moved to France 'cause mum reckoned she could get me better treatment there. And she was right.'

Going to France was the most difficult time in Mel's life. Having lived in London all her life she suddenly found herself in a small French village 'full of old men' and she couldn't speak a word of French.

'It was just great,' she deadpans. 'It was like, in England I'd been a nerd at primary school, and then I got to French school and I was a freak because I wasn't French. The kids there were so different. Everybody there wanted to be a doctor or a vet or something, and I'd just come from this stage school where everyone wanted to be a star.'

But, like everything else, Mel soon got used to it and, more importantly, she had her operation.

'We saw a couple of specialists in France and there was

> 11 <

one that was perfect so we went ahead with the op. They put three metal rods in my back to keep it straight — it wasn't painful actually. I was just glad I was getting fixed.

'So I have these metal hooks in my back now, which clip my back together,' she explains. 'So, when I go through customs at airports I usually set off the metal detectors. I'm like, is it my jewellery, is it my watch? And then I remember.'

Life in France had its advantages, not least the fact that Mel soon became fluent in her mother's language (a great asset in European interviews!). Her education blossomed, she got herself a good gang of mates and she no longer felt lost in France. But despite it all, she still had a bit of an urge to sing.

'I did a bit of acting in France to make a bit of cash — just a couple of things, nothing special (no, I'm not going to say!) but there was nothing for me in France, musically. I wanted to do music, I don't really like the acting thing, so I thought, "Right. back to England."

'It was just one of those things,' she grins. 'I came to England to stay with a friend and within a month I was singing with a band. I was soooo lucky.'

She didn't think it was so peachy at the time: her boyfriend was supposed to be following her to England. Did he come? Did he heck...

'He was a cretin!' she laughs. 'I went back to France about, oh, three months later and there he was going out with some other girl called Melanie! And he was only fifteen! Can you believe that?'

Not that she cared for long. Once Mel kicked off her singing career in London she found herself in what Shaznay describes as 'that London music circuit thing' — meeting one group of musicians who introduced her to another and then another — and then she met Shaznay...

Within months she was heading up a band, Drive, who were signed to the One Little Indian label ('we released a single and it did nothing') and then Mel met a DJ called Jay Strongman who formed a group

'I had no bad subjects at school. I was okay at everything — except sport. I'm terrible at sport, I just can't do it. During cross-country running I used to wear these two-tone winklepickers, with leggings and my mum's big orange jumper. I'd always come last in the races and I wouldn't mind at all. I've got no sense of competition where that's concerned. Yep, sport was definitely my worst subject.'

with Mel, his girlfriend and a drummer. Mel was well up for it.

'It was a bit of a weird time but it was also very exciting,' she remembers. 'I lived with them for a bit and then I got involved in Dreadzone, which was cool. [Mel actually appeared on Dreadzone's first album in 1995, appearing on TV with them as a backing singer alongside Denise Van Outen.]

'I didn't know anyone when I started out but then you meet someone and that's it! I was hanging around in the Metamorphosis studio when I finally met Shaznay about two years later. And that's how all this began.'

Maybe Mel's tricky past has toughened her up (it can't have been a breeze facing paralysis, changing schools, having to learn another language...) but whatever — she's definitely the Saint who doesn't suffer fools gladly.

'I am the least trusting one in the band,' she says seriously. 'I think I've just been burned so badly in the past, y'know, with people that you think are there to help you and then you find out that they're not all that. So, yeah, I suppose I am kind of tough really. And I won't stick anyone who patronises me. If anyone thinks I'm a girl and I don't know anything then they're just looking for a fight.'

Mel Blatt certainly means business at work. Turns out she means business in the kitchen too. When she's not rehearsing, touring, recording or doing interviews she chills out, mostly by watching telly.

*Eastenders* and *The O Zone* figure high on her viewing stats but pride of place goes to *Ready Steady Cook*.

'Yeah, 'cause I love cooking!' she laughs. '*Ready Steady Cook* is my favourite programme ever. Nic took me to watch it being filmed once and it was just brilliant ... although I can't remember what they cooked.'

So what can she cook?

'Anything, mate! Meatballs, fondue, fish... Listen, I'm a great cook! I'm the chef of the band — I think that's the French side of me coming out.'

*Naturellement!*

As well as being band chef then, Mel has a couple of other strings to her bow, as Nic explains: 'Mel's the band nurse. No — the pharmacist!' she laughs. 'It's like, if you ask her for anything she'll have it in her bag — aspirin, Elastoplast, chewing gum; whatever you want, she'll have it. She's the organiser, in a way. She's wise and great at sorting out problems but she's also a bit of a nutter — and she likes banter!'

Mel agrees with this assessment. 'Oh yeah. I'll argue with anyone.' She shrugs her shoulders. 'I do like a banter — just love seeing how far I can push people before they can crack. People always look at me as if to say "You're a nutter, mate" but I don't care, 'cause it's true! I do have my peaceful moments though.'

She pauses.

'No, I do!'

# SHAZNAY

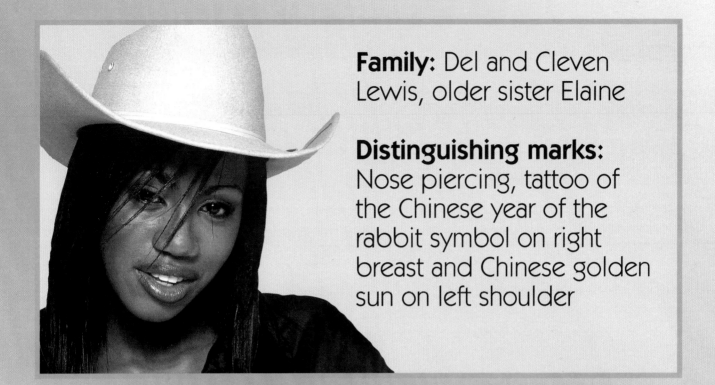

**Family:** Del and Cleven Lewis, older sister Elaine

**Distinguishing marks:** Nose piercing, tattoo of the Chinese year of the rabbit symbol on right breast and Chinese golden sun on left shoulder

'I was born on 14 October 1975 in Islington, north London, to Del and Cleven Lewis. I've lived there all my life. My mum works with kids and my dad used to be a bus driver but he isn't any more.

'My first memory is watching my sister leave to go to school in her green uniform. She's called Elaine and she's twelve years older than me. I've got a nephew, her son, Leon – and he's like a brother to me. He's seventeen now.

'In the house my parents played a lot of Bob Marley and Johnny Mathis, I remember I used to sing along – I think I was taken by Johnny Mathis's lyrics in "When a Child is Born". The first record I bought was Bill Ocean's "When the Going Gets Tough". I always wanted to sing.'

# T LEWIS

'I am the quietest of the group but around people who know me I seem like the loudest. Saying that, I think I've become quieter in the past few months because of being in the group.'

'I can't get my head around any of this. I can't get to grips with how big it is. It's like, I walked down Oxford Street the other day with dirty hair and I suddenly thought, am I allowed to walk around looking this bad? I go to pick my nose and I have to stop myself. Pop stars don't do that, do they? It's mad.'

When Shaznay Lewis first uttered these words, she had no idea just how much madder it would

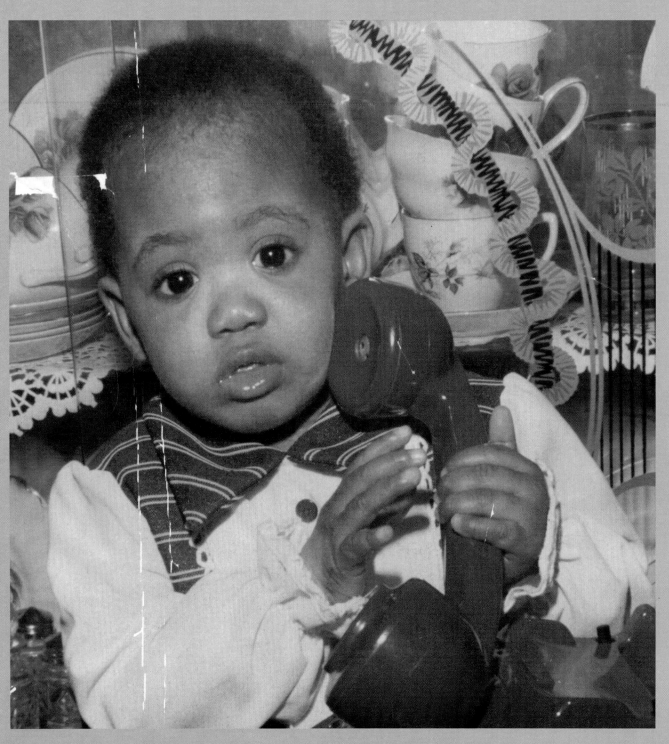

get. Sitting wrapped up on the set of a video shoot, Shaznay was recovering from flu just weeks after 'I Know Where It's At' had entered the charts. She was literally delirious!

Shaznay knew something big was happening, was almost fazed by it, but all she could do was giggle at 'the weirdness of it'. As the other girls wandered around in their curlers (Mel whipping up toasted peanut butter and jelly sandwiches, while Nic and Nat teased tour manager John Buckland about his down-to-the-detail organisational skills), Shaznay hibernated in her parka, the hood pulled over her eyes, as she chatted about her new-found success. 'It's weird. It really is weird.'

The weirdest part of it, in reality, is that Shaznay's fame has been such a long time coming.

Even though she's still only twenty-three, Shaznay T. Lewis has already notched up an 'established' musical career, a career which began when she was a nipper, playing at being a DJ.

The north London girl, daughter of a Jamaican mum and Barbadian dad, was set on being a music maestro. She would spend days in her Islington family home, sitting in her bedroom manning the turntables of her imaginary decks. 'I'd pretend to be the DJ introducing a record, y'see,' she explains. 'And then I wouldn't have the record so I'd have to

pretend to be the record. So I taped myself singing everything from Madonna to Whitney Houston.'

Otherwise she developed into a pretty ordinary London teenager, hanging out with her mates and working hard at school. She was brought up with a sound religious background ('but my mum wasn't a Bible-basher or anything like that') and went to a church school (mainly, she laughs, to check out the altar boys). She was rarely in trouble — her one notable run in at school involved her lassooing a lad with a skipping rope (he'd picked on her) — and got on pretty well with her elder sister Elaine, who's twelve years older ('we had one row which lasted for ages until my mum sorted it out'). The girl didn't need trouble to make her life interesting — she had hobbies for that: a stint with Arsenal girls' football club (even though she's a Spurs supporter) and, most memorably, her music.

'I used to go to a youth club and I learnt to play the drums. I still play a bit — I'm good at it — I'm no Phil Collins, but I'm okay. I've always been a beats person — much more into beats than melodies really — so the drums and the piano are the only instruments that I could ever get into. That was kind of like my first attempt at writing anything musical.'

Meanwhile Shaznay was preparing for her first public singing performance.

'Ah yeah,' says Shaznay. 'Er, this is what happened. I was always the one in the yard getting all my mates to learn to do dance routines and stuff. One year we had this summer fête and we asked our headmistress if we could do a little routine at it. She said yeah so we chose to perform Five Star's "If I Say Yes". We got our mums to go down to Marks and Spencers and we got these beige outfits — cord trousers, T-shirts and white trainers — and looked brilliant. We were good!'

Shaznay's spirit was knocked a bit when she was eleven and had to leave primary school to go to senior school.

'The worst five years of my life,' she states unhappily. 'I converted to being a Catholic and then I went to a school called Mount Carmel. I made great friends but I didn't like it at all. I was an English boffin and I was into dance and sports but I wasn't too keen on maths.

'This is great but it's not the way I imagined it. In the beginning it was just us doing our stuff but now it's so much more about business. I never thought I'd be doing so much — not just performing but promotion and travelling. We're getting used to it now but at the end of the day the whole point of it for me is to write songs and perform.'

'I used to sit at the back of the French class and fall asleep. I never used to go to assembly, I always used to go and sit on the toilet for half an hour and listen to my Walkman and read *Smash Hits* until it was over.'

A couple of years into senior school, Shaznay wrote her first song, 'Just My Luck'.

'Do I remember it? Yeah. Can I remember the lyrics? Nooooo. I'm not telling you. It was about love and I knew nothing about love when I was thirteen! It was all right. Don't think it'll be appearing on the next album or anythin', but it was okay for thirteen!'

Shaznay continued with the songwriting and by the time she was fifteen she was entering music competitions, looking for a foothold in the music industry. She studied music, photography and English, placing emphasis on her music work.

'I'd walk around with a rucksack full of lyrics and tapes (much like now) and was pretty single-minded about what I wanted to do. Actually, I've still got my music exam work tucked away at home somewhere. It sounds like, er, exam work! The keyboards are really tinkly.'

Shaznay moved on to Westminster College, to study business, but while she was there she kept writing, listening and learning, trying to find a way into her chosen career. Her biggest break, however, came purely by accident at a party, when she bumped into 80s popstar Ben from Curiosity Killed the Cat.

Shaznay's mates, all rooting for her music career, spotted Ben at the do and told him that Shaznay was a talented vocalist. Ben got interested, had a chat to her about her work and then said, 'Right then. Let's go down the studio and see what you're made of.'

Shaznay was a bit worried that it might be a dodgy situation, but her mates encouraged her and she went to Metamorphosis the next day to meet Ben.

'He just flung this instrumental record on and said "Sing" so I started singing to the backing track and they went "Cor!"

'When I was in primary school I was interested in poetry and I still love the whole idea of rhyming, someone talking about a subject. You know they get those funky rappers, they stand and rap about anything? I'm fascinated by that. It's one of the reasons I started writing because I love the whole idea of rhyming. It's nicer when it's something that means something and it's true and it's a story.'

Without realising it, Shaznay had got what she'd been looking for — a ticket into the music biz.

'You get to this stage where you find yourself constantly being in a circle of aspiring musicians and that's what happened to me,' she explains. 'I ended up working a lot at Metamorphosis, which, of course, is where I met Mel. After a while it all kind of fell into place that it was me and Mel working together.'

So that was that for Miss Lewis. At one point she did attempt to have a 'proper job' — working in a men's clothing store in north London — but it wasn't her scene. She did a three-week stint there, filling in for a friend, and was so good that they offered her a permanent position — but Shaznay politely declined. ('I was in the shoe department and I spent all day giving out refunds,' Shaznay told *FHM*. This wasn't the kind of soul Ms Lewis was interested in.) 'Shaznay,' says Nic, 'is the quiet one of All Saints. She's the shyest really.'

Shaznay agrees. 'I am,' she admits. 'I have my moments, though. I can be a bit mad like the others, but I'm probably the most serious.'

She is also the sexiest, if you believe the journalists who meet her. Tagged '0891 Saint' by *Sky* for her sexy voice and 'unquestionably sexy' by *FHM*, she's been given her fair share of attention by male pop stars the band now meet.

Shaznay finds it hysterically funny. 'No!' she howls, 'I can't believe people say that about me. Really?' And she flushes with embarrassment.

She just can't see it herself. To her, she's just Shaznay, the girl who eats at Burger King and McDonald's, thinks nothing's better than snuggling up under the duvet and watching Ricki Lake ('I'm the patron saint of watching soaps') and wore a brace for two years ('It didn't bother me at all 'cause I know it's doing me good in the long run').

Basically, Shaznay doesn't care about the stuff that comes with fame (apart from, perhaps, the Calvin Klein wardrobe). What she's most interested in is the job itself — the songwriting and, even more, the performing.

'I love going on stage and performing in front of a crowd,' she says. 'It's like, sometimes we travel a long way, and we go on stage, and it's over in a few minutes and I feel a bit sad.'

Her least favourite part of the job is travelling: '...'cause I hate flying.'

What sums up Shaznay the most is probably this: In December last year, before 'Never Ever' made the number-one slot, *Top Of The Pops* magazine hit Shaznay with the ultimate question: If it all went wrong, if All Saints wasn't happening, what would Shaznay be doing? Her answer: 'I'd be singing on my own.'

She smiles. 'This is what I've been striving for. The other day I was reading my school leaving book and one of my friends had written, "Hope to see you on *Top Of The Pops*." My life revolves around music. It's what I'm all about...'

NICOLE

**Nickname:** Nicky, Nic, or The Fonz.

**Family:** She's the youngest of three sisters: Nat, Lori and Lee. Her mum is called Mary and her dad is Ken.

**Distinguishing marks:** Chinese year of the tiger symbol tattoo on her waist and a belly piercing ('which an old hippy did for me').

'I was born in 1974 on 7 December in Hamilton, Canada. We moved to Toronto soon after so I don't remember Hamilton at all. I was a happy child, one of those ones who used to get up at 7 a.m. to go swimming all the time. I probably annoyed everybody. All I can remember of being really young is being jealous of my three sisters, who went to school. I was looked after by a lady who had a child the same age as me. She never paid me any attention and made me sit in her daughter's room all day while she and her daughter watched telly.

'There's four of us: me, Nat, Lori and Lee. Lori has just come over from the States and Lee works for a publishing company. They both live in Camden, north London. My parents, Mary and Ken, live in London too.'

# MARIE APPLETON

icole Appleton was once working at an outdoor ice-cream kiosk in New York when a gust of wind blew over the kiosk brolly, and knocked her out cold. Apparently $90 worth of ice-cream got stolen while she lay unconscious, so she got sacked. So much for the ice-cream business.

In her time, Nic's also scraped a living as a waitress, a bartender and a lifeguard (where, legend dubiously has it, she saved an otter's life) but ... she got sacked from those jobs too. So it's just as well that none of them suited her as much as her present job. Nic does makes a rather good Saint.

'Got any gossip?'

Nicole Appleton bounds over in her big chunky parka and administers a big hug, ears at the ready. If Shaz is sexy, Nat's honest and Mel's down to earth and sultry, Nic is definitely the friendliest Saint. Talk to starry-eyed male journalists who meet her and they all say the same thing: she's great for a chat.

Nic grew up as the youngest of four daughters in the Appleton household. Lori and Lee, the eldest, had already progressed to make-up and boyfriends when she was a kid, so she generally ended up hanging out with Nat, the next youngest of her siblings.

She had a pretty idyllic childhood.

'When I was young, when I first went to school, I loved it,' she remembers.

'I used to love things like Halloween. It's very big in the States and Canada. If you've ever seen

'When I was ten my mum bought a turquoise caravan for us to take on holiday. I remember camping in a field of cows and thinking it was really cool. When we came back from holiday the van sat outside our house and all my friends would play in it. It was like my own Wendy House.'

*ET*, where they all walk around dressed up, that's exactly what it was like in my town. I once dressed up as a witch and won a competition for best costume because my older sister Lee knew about make-up and everything. I was only about five but I wore a big skirt over my head and Lee sprayed my hair green and painted my face green. No other kid had that!'

'I was great at everything in school. The only thing that I hated was reading, especially reading aloud. I was a tomboy. I spent my time climbing trees, hanging out with the boys, building camps and cutting my hair short. I wore jeans instead of dresses and every time we played *Grease* I played Danny because I was a tomboy. What else do I remember...? Oh, I remember my first mate, who was a boy who lived in the same block of flats as us. He was such a nerd. Vidak, he was called. All I can remember really is that he had a fish tank and there were so many fish in it they couldn't move.'

When Nic was about five or six, her parents

separated. Both her parents are English, and after due consideration Nic's dad moved back to England to settle in his mother country. A while later the Appletons' mum decided to move back too, and both parents ended up living together to bring the girls up.

It was then that the showbiz thing began for Nicole...

'I loved dancing, you see...' Nic explains, '...and my mum thought that maybe it was worth me giving stage school a try (it was either that or private school and when I went to sit the test for that, all the girls seemed really posh; I didn't fit in). I did an audition for the Sylvia Young Theatre School. I was so excited! I was supposed to have something rehearsed and all I did was a cartwheel! Anyway I got accepted.'

Nicole was seven when she first started her training (Natalie joined her a year later) and, in the beginning she realy enjoyed it.

Within a week she'd met Mel and it was obvious from the very beginning that they'd be friends for a long time.

'We got on right from the start,' Nic smiles. 'We were always good friends and always together. We had such a laugh.'

Nic did a bit of movie work — as an extra in *Brazil* and *Santa Claus the Movie* — and had a pretty good time of it. It wasn't all roses though. The way Mel and Nic are now you'd have thought they'd have ruled the school. Unfortunately nothing was further from the truth.

'Suddenly there was this thing about popularity at school,' Nic explains. 'It seemed to me that it got to the point where, if you weren't blonde with lipstick, you weren't going to get anywhere. We were just normal kids — brown eyes, brown hair, dull looking, and they didn't give us the time of day. It really left a mark on me and I lost all confidence by the time I left.

'The funny thing is that every popular kid at school is doing nothing now. When I met Mel we stuck together for the whole year we were together and we got called nerds. So Mel said, "Okay, you're the Fonz" to make me seem cool and it's stuck ever since.'

Despite the traumas, Mel and Nic really didn't

care. They were mates, which is what counted, and they were probably more interested in having a laugh than making it into the cast of *Friends*. Of course, with Mel's health problems their friendship was brought to an abrupt halt after a year ... and then the Appleton family upped sticks and moved to New York. Nic was devastated about leaving at first, but the move did have its advantages: suddenly the popularity issue wasn't a problem.

'People liked me and wanted to talk to me because I was English,' she laughs. 'I got into sports and became a cheerleader. I loved it — when you're fourteen it's quite exciting. I went out with the best-looking football player in school (although he's lost everything now and I'm embarrassed to admit he was my boyfriend — but he was so good looking and so great at football).

'I really changed actually. I became blonde, got a suntan very quickly and was just accepted. It was great.'

Nic was almost sixteen when the Appletons moved yet again — this time it was a two-month stint in Fort Lauderdale, Florida. It was only two months because, when Nic's mum tried to enrol her in a school, she was sent a list of things that kids couldn't take to class — 'knives, machine guns, machetes...') and, not surprisingly, Nic refused to set foot in the place. Time to get out the suitcases again, then. Britain here we come...

'I remember I just announced that I was going back to England to live with Nat and that was that,' Nic grins. 'We lived in a flat in Camden Lock and I started going out. At sixteen I was blonde and I thought I could do whatever I wanted. I went out to clubs, met a lot of crazy people and did some crazy things. I thought I was very mature.'

After a few summers back in New York making money doing odd jobs (hence the ice-cream shenanigans) and singing with Nat, Nic finally settled in London for good just before she turned twenty.

She didn't know it then, but Mel was about to re-enter her life and save her from a pretty unsavoury situation.

'Here's what happened: I moved back to London and got involved in a relationship straight away. I couldn't describe the guy except that he was the worst person in the world.

'I'm the life
and soul of
the group.'

'He was a big druggie, a horrible person.

'He took care of me, gave me everything, immediately – he was very wealthy – but he made me stay up at weekends with him and I went so downhill. It ruined me for a year. He totally brain-washed me.

'Anyway, towards the end of the relationship I ran into Mel. I couldn't have found a better person to take me away from all of that. I told her about him and she was saying, "I'm going to kill him!" ... he was getting abusive.

'Anyway, after that year – which is a complete blur to me – I became dedicated to the group. I didn't want to do anything else...'

And that's where the All Saints story begins for Nic.

Nic and Mel are still the most inseparable of the All Saints girls – pulling faces at each other in meetings and larking about in photoshoots, despite the hard work that they seem to sail through.

They've been through hard times – including poverty and near starvation – but they've always believed in and stood up for each other.

'Nic's been my best mate for ever,' Mel says. And it's easy to see why. She's so cheery she'd put even the grumpiest person into a good mood. As Nic told *Smash Hits* last year, she's definitely the 'life and soul' of the group.

'I guess I am,' she admits. 'Even when they [the rest of the band] are in a bad mood I cheer them up.'

That doesn't mean she's sweetness and light all the time. She is up for a good row every now and then. 'I like getting everything off my chest,' she grins. 'If I start rowing with my male friends they'll say, "Oh, look at you trying to be Miss Bossy Boots all of a sudden." I'll be like, yeah, you're right. I don't like being that type of person. Sometimes I need to be put in my place.'

When Nic gets a day off (and that's not often – she didn't get a day off for three months after the release of 'I Know Where It's At'!) she tends to relax in a down-beat kind of way. She's not really a clubby girl – she thinks nothing's better than clothes shopping, or vegging with a video (her favourite being *Fried Green Tomatoes At The Whistlestop Café*). Generally, she just likes to hang out.

'I'm comfortable. I just chill and watch TV and do what I want,' she laughs. 'I walk around the house with nothing on if I feel like it. But I also like being with people, especially cool people. By that I mean people who are down to earth, who can have a good laugh and a good old gossip.'

And gossip is what she does best! Nic's a people person. She's the first to come over and chat with anyone who's feeling left out of a situation and is always ready for a good chinwag. Chatting is her forte, and she's renowned for spending ages answering journos' questions. On one occasion, when a journalist was interviewing all four All Saints at the same time, Nat asked if Nic could answer her questions later 'or we'll be here all day!' she grinned.

Maybe it's her chatting skills that make her seem so friendly — possibly it's her big beaming smile — but whatever it is, Nic is definitely a popular All Saint. Has she a bad bone in her body?

'Of course,' she says. 'But the thing about us is that when we sin, we sin in a Saintly way...'

Hmmmmm. That'll be it.

'We're not good all the time, you know. We do get a bit bored sometimes and get up to mischief. Like, Mel sending all the hotel towels down to the lobby in the elevator. Or the time Nat and Shaznay got called over the tannoy at the airport because they'd written the initials AS in the back of a plane seat. We're having competitions at the moment to see who can smuggle out the biggest thing from a hotel — not expensive things, just stupid things. I think I'm winning — I smuggled out a bud vase...'

# NATALIE

**Nickname:** Fat Cat, from being a chubby baby.

**Family:** Daughter Rachel, sister Nicole, Lori and Lee (Nat's the second youngest).

**Distinguishing marks:** Red Canadian Maple leaf in a private place.

'I was born in Canada in Mississauga, 14 May 1973. As a kid I was the boss. I bossed Nicky around. I used to make her do everything for me. If I was on the toilet and I needed toilet roll I would make her get it. If we had Neopolitan ice-cream I'd have the chocolate and the strawberry and make her have only the vanilla. Still, Nicky was my best friend.'

# JANE APPLETON

**N**at Appleton is walking around with curlers in her hair. And she still looks gorgeous. Collapsing on the end of a bench, surrounded by cushions, the tiny Saint is laughing about her hairdo, trying to explain to someone what the curlers in her hair actually do (doh?) while fielding calls on her mobile phone.

She's getting ready for a video shoot, hence much to'ing and fro'ing to the make-up artist's chair, but putting on showbiz glamour is something Nat's well used to. She's been doing it since her teens.

Rewind a few years, to a hotel in New York, where a young female singer is about to take the stage. Despite an 'awful keyboard player' the dolled-up babe begins her set singing a handful of popular songs with the Safari Lounge Band — belting

out everything from Madonna to Whitney Houston. She's pretty good and gets a great reception. It's no wonder that the hotel staff have absolutely no idea that... she's only fifteen. Ladies and gents, you're watching a young Nat Appleton at the beginning of her singing career.

'They really did have no idea how old I was,' Nat laughs, recalling her hotel singing days. 'But I was safe. My mum used to dress me up to help me look older and then I'd sing — in respectable hotels in the Catskills, where Danny Kaye started out! I'd sing "Tie A Yellow Ribbon",

'At school I was a maths whizz. My books would be sent to the principal to sign them and to show parents. I wanted to be a doctor or a dentist because I was fascinated with teeth. I used to get my mum's encyclopedias and take them out and look at all the teeth and draw them, at seven years old. Actually I was a very logical kid. I used to figure out my mum's problems by moving her furniture around.'

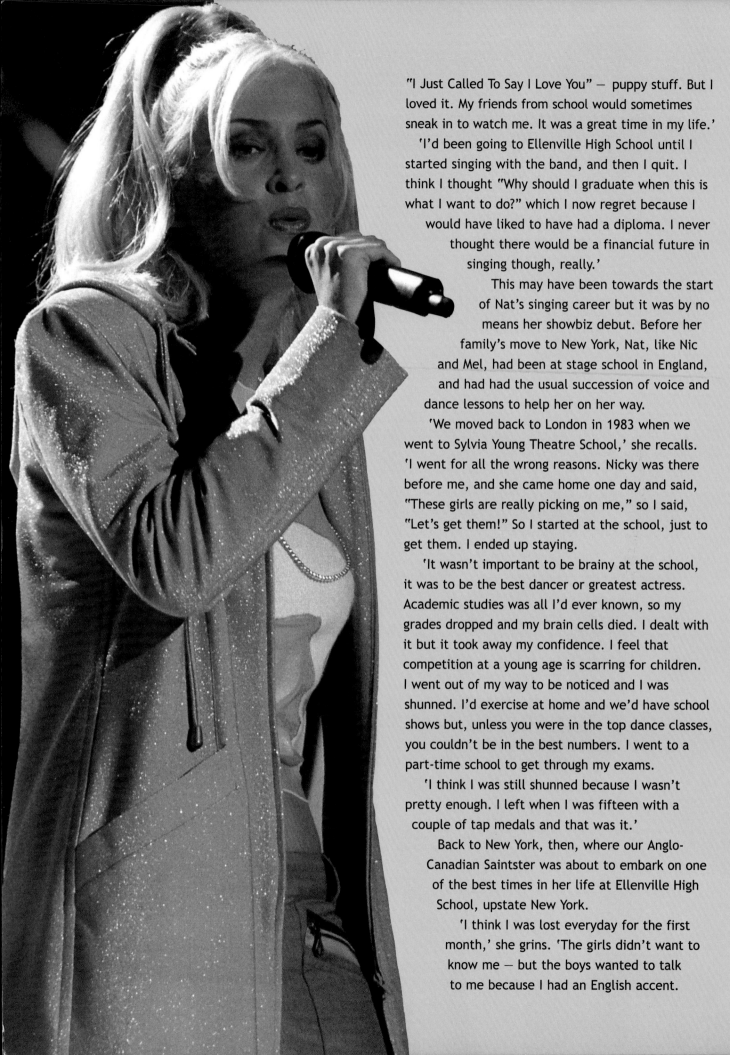

"I Just Called To Say I Love You" — puppy stuff. But I loved it. My friends from school would sometimes sneak in to watch me. It was a great time in my life.'

'I'd been going to Ellenville High School until I started singing with the band, and then I quit. I think I thought "Why should I graduate when this is what I want to do?" which I now regret because I would have liked to have had a diploma. I never thought there would be a financial future in singing though, really.'

This may have been towards the start of Nat's singing career but it was by no means her showbiz debut. Before her family's move to New York, Nat, like Nic and Mel, had been at stage school in England, and had had the usual succession of voice and dance lessons to help her on her way.

'We moved back to London in 1983 when we went to Sylvia Young Theatre School,' she recalls. 'I went for all the wrong reasons. Nicky was there before me, and she came home one day and said, "These girls are really picking on me," so I said, "Let's get them!" So I started at the school, just to get them. I ended up staying.

'It wasn't important to be brainy at the school, it was to be the best dancer or greatest actress. Academic studies was all I'd ever known, so my grades dropped and my brain cells died. I dealt with it but it took away my confidence. I feel that competition at a young age is scarring for children. I went out of my way to be noticed and I was shunned. I'd exercise at home and we'd have school shows but, unless you were in the top dance classes, you couldn't be in the best numbers. I went to a part-time school to get through my exams.

'I think I was still shunned because I wasn't pretty enough. I left when I was fifteen with a couple of tap medals and that was it.'

Back to New York, then, where our Anglo-Canadian Saintster was about to embark on one of the best times in her life at Ellenville High School, upstate New York.

'I think I was lost everyday for the first month,' she grins. 'The girls didn't want to know me — but the boys wanted to talk to me because I had an English accent.

'I don't know if it was love but my first proper boyfriend was a guy called Tony. He was the biggest football player in the team and he drove a nice sports car. He was nice. We did the usual stuff: drive-in movies, went to see the mountains, the waterfall... He was the biggest boy in Ellenville High. I'd see him have fights in the football field and he would pick up guys and throw them. No one would mess with Tony!'

A couple of months down the line I made friends though. I was a cheerleader too.'

When she wasn't making money singing, or hanging out with her new friends, Nat was having great success in a field she'd never really dabbled in before: BOYS! In England she 'couldn't get arrested' when it came to men — her love life had been totally non-existent — but then she parked-up in the US and — weyhey! — it was party time.

'I had the choice, sweetie,' she laughs. 'I went from being an ugly duck in England, when I was desperate to have anyone, to being able to have anyone in New York. I dyed my hair red, turned into Tiffany [an 80s pop star] and, er, that was that.'

Things couldn't get any better. Life was as exciting as it gets for Nat. She spent the next couple of years racing around having a great time — at one point even running aerobics lessons — and then things changed dramatically.

After living for a short time in Florida, Nat moved back to England to live in Camden, where she met a dancer, Carl Robinson. Nat picks up the story ...

'I was seventeen and he was a stripper, five years older than me. I met him at a show — I was only young for godsakes! At seventeen all that matters is looks. Anyway, I got pregnant and had a daughter, Rachel, in 1991, when I was eighteen.

'When she was three months old we thought we'd go and live in America. We had a daughter so I was determined to make it work for her sake. Me — fool, alien citizen who's Canadian — thought if we got married he could work there. So we did and I went to immigration in New York City and they said, "Sorry, he's not acceptable," so I became a wifey for nothing!'

Unfortunately the relationship soon broke down. Carl returned to England because he couldn't make any money and Nat followed a few months later to have their marriage annulled. In other words, contrary to reports in tabloid newspapers, Nat is not married.

'Rachel was the only thing holding us together,' she states. 'I didn't make sure Carl would make payments. I just trusted that he would, so I didn't get it in writing. He never gave anything, never phoned. It freaks me out.'

'My daughter, Rachel, loves the band, and in one way she thinks it's great because she's very popular but in one way that upsets me because I don't want her getting special treatment because of that. Sometimes we'll put a video on or something and she won't want to watch it and then I know there's something seriously up. I worry about her a lot. I love her so much and obviously I want her to be happy and I want her to be her own person.'

Luckily Nat went to New York again, had 'one of the best summers of my life' and then came back to England again in 1996.

'My parents looked after Rachel for a while so I could get my life together. I moved in with Nicky in Camden and got my life back on track. I felt like I'd missed out on so much, that I was getting back the years I'd missed. That's when the band happened. By Christmas we'd got the deal and my parents moved over with Rachel the following year.'

Nat is now happy — if exhausted — doing the only thing she's ever wanted to do.

She's bright — sharp — a little unromantic but a lot of fun.

('What would you like your book to be like?' I asked her. 'Big. With crosswords. And dot-to-dot. Lots of dot-to-dot,' she deadpanned.)

While she'll confess to being a worrier she does tend to let her hair down big time on the ten days a year she's actually at home.

'I used to be more outrageous but I can't do the things I used to,' she explains. 'I used to be outrageous, wild and outgoing, but when I get home I just want to be normal and do normal things again. I get to see friends so rarely because if I get two days off a month it's for my child and my boyfriend.'

One of her favourite ways of winding down is reading horror books.

'I have to have my horror,' she grins. 'I can't go without it. I'll come home at one in the morning and I'll still have to read for half an hour before I go to sleep.'

Is she sick?

She laughs. 'Perhaps I am. I don't know why I love it, I just do. I watched horror films from the age of seven. And I guess I like it because it's completely not normal. It takes me away from life completely. The vomiting, the heads spinning. I like that stuff. It's not real, is it?'

Despite her 'eclectic' tastes, Nat is an extremely approachable Saint. As she herself has said, she's definitely friendly and outgoing (as well as painfully honest) but her Achilles heel is her perfectionism — which goes hand in hand with bossiness!

'I'm the big sister of the group,' she says. 'I boss everyone around... I do like to have my own way. That's the Taurus in me. I'm always right and I'll argue to the death.'

She's also got a very quick temper on her, and very little patience. 'True,' she says. 'If I'm in a queue and the person in front takes out a credit card just to buy a pair of socks, it'll be like World Ward III is about to start.'

Despite that, Nic says Nat's been a great sister, even if she has been a little overprotective sometimes.

'I'm very much the protective big sister,' Nat smiles. 'In recent years I've become a lot better. As soon as Nic was dating a guy I didn't like, I was on her back like a rash. Now I let her do her own thing and make her own mistakes.'

That's pretty much Nat's own outlook on life now: do what you do — and then learn from it.

Nat, still in her early twenties, has had enough experiences for one lifetime: she's travelled the world, had a number-one record and, most preciously, has a daughter. She obviously has nothing to regret.

'Y'know what?' she says. 'I believe the best way to learn is through your own mistakes and experiences. Just always be yourself.'

# THE NATIVITY

**W**hen Shaznay met Mel she'd already been carving out a career for herself in the backing vocals trade. Ever since that night when she'd met Ben from Curiosity she'd found herself on a musical roller-coaster, being recommended from contact to contact until she'd become quite a well-known name in certain musical circles.

By the time she crossed paths with Mel, at Metamorphosis, Shaznay was pretty much a fixture at the studio, but had ambitions of doing more than just singing back-up. She wanted to record her own stuff. She already had almost a library of songs and ideas for tracks filed away to record, but needed studio time to get them into a presentable demo state. At the studio she was on to a winner: Shaznay was singing for little-known old-school hip-hop artist Rodney C, in return for free studio time. It was a deal which kept both parties happy.

Mel, meanwhile, was on a learning curve, treating the studio as a kind of street university. For two years she hung out there, studying the techniques and tactics of singing, recording and songwriting, but to begin with she hardly sang a note: she restricted her work to 'observing' and 'just making tea'.

'It's completely sad,' she told *Vox*, 'but that's not the point. I'd just sit on the couch and listen and hear what was going on. I wouldn't ask for anything, I wasn't being paid, I was just making tea. I was nothing. Eventually I did backing vocals for people, but that was it for two years.'

The pair progressed with their musical studies (Ms Lewis scoring an ace in 1992 when she performed with Double Trouble at the Hammersmith Palais) but it took a while for Mel and Shaznay to forge a friendship. If anything, Mel was in awe.

'I remember seeing Shaznay for the first time at Metamorphosis,' she remembers. 'She came in with loads of mates. I didn't have any friends at the time — especially not girlfriends. But I thought she was stunning. Then I heard her do a cover of an old Jimmy Cliff song and I thought, "Wow!".

Shaznay's first reaction towards Mel was pretty much one of indifference.

'When I first saw Mel she was sitting in the studio talking to Don, the singer,' Shaznay remembers.

'She was talking about changing the colour of her hair and was sitting there like this [pretends to be demure] looking at her nails. I never spoke to her until one of the guys at the studio asked me and Mel to do some backing vocals on someone's track. That's really when I started talking to her.'

Hanging out together, they realised that they shared musical tastes as well as their sense of humour, and so they started working together —

writing, recording and producing their own tracks for demo. The pair worked so well together that their partnership developed into a band, incorporating a third member, Simone Rainford.

Things moved pretty quickly for the girls. They soon found themselves signed to ZTT, the label owned by pop's Mr Production, Trevor Sheen. It was amazing: they had a proper record contract!

It was an exciting time. Shaznay and Mel were still extremely young and the experience of being able to actually record proper in-your-record-shop CDs at such a young age must have been very welcome. But something was wrong.

When the girls' first and only single, 'If You Wanna Party', was spawned, it launched itself with a nose-dive straight into the reject bin. This wasn't in the plan.

'We didn't know what direction we wanted to go in and ZTT didn't really know what to do with us,' Mel explained later. 'It was a pretty short-lived thing. Our one release was deleted very quickly.'

The single a no-go, Rainford left, and Mel and Shaznay parted company with their record label. As quickly as it had begun, their first relationship with a major record company was over.

Perhaps the reason that the deal didn't work was the thing that makes All Saints so different from their contemporaries: the girls wanted to do *their* thing, and nobody else's.

'From the start we just wanted to do our own thing,' says Shaznay. 'We've been very single-minded about what we wanted to sound like and how we wanted to be put across. We always had that thing where guys would approach us in the street and say "Wanna be in my band? I'm looking for a singer."'

The girls just weren't interested. They wanted more of a say in what kind of band they were, they wanted to have some influence in the direction their music should take, and being a mouthpiece for another bunch of musicians was not where it was at. They wanted — needed — full control. As Shaznay explains: 'We weren't interested in dancing to some producer's tune.'

Back to the drawing board, then. While their first record-releasing experience may have been slightly disheartening, Shaznay and Mel were grounded in their self-belief and were determined to find some way of forging a career on their own terms, so they pressed on.

'It was strange when the ZTT thing fell through. We'd worked hard to get a deal so I suppose we should have been gutted but we weren't really. I suppose our main feeling was relief. It was just a release. The whole thing just didn't work. I remember we did the Smash Hits tour in '95 and we could see looking around us that we were being treated so differenty to the other acts on tour – even the new groups like us – that we felt something was seriously wrong. We just didn't have the support or, at least, we knew that what we wanted was entirely different to what ZTT wanted. Anyway, the day that we left was actually quite good in that respect. It just meant that we could start again. We were disappointed, yeah, but we didn't even think of giving in.'

*Shaznay*

'I remember meeting up with Shaz and Mel when we first talked about me joining All Saints. Mel was saying Shaz didn't get along with a lot of people, she was a bit shy, but we got on like a house on fire. We met at TGI Friday's in Leicester Square in the West End. Mel and I went out for a drink and Shaz came along. We all got a bit drunk. I couldn't ask for someone better than Mel to ask me to join a band. I always wanted to do it, I was like "yeah" without even hesitating.'

*Nic*

'I've good memories from Metamorphosis – I've also got bad ones though. But it was a good experience. I learned a lot about music and artists and creativity and being inspired by the talent that was around me. That's what I got from it. But I also became less trusting of people and, again, that's where my cynicism started really.

Metamorphosis isn't around any more and I don't really see any of the people who used to hang out there. I mean, there are people like Don and a couple of other musicians that I became friends with who I see occasionally. And they're all doing fine.'

*Mel*

As they continued, they reached a point where they realised that they still needed a third voice to add to the group, but were wary of trawling through a tiresome auditioning process to find that added factor. Shaznay picks up the story:

'We felt that it would be nice to have one more member of the group but we didn't want to audition anyone as we needed someone who completely understood our music as well as being able to sing,' she explains. 'When we bumped into Nicky and heard her sing we knew right away she would be perfect.'

As corny as the phrase 'fate intervened' may sound, that's exactly what happened.

Nic, freshly returned from New York, was out and about in London one day when she bumped into Mel's dad. In the course of their conversation, Mr Blatt told Nicky what his daughter was up to these days; Nic was immediately interested in finding out more. With Mel's dad's help the childhood mates renewed contact and, of course, Mel introduced Nic to Shaznay. It was obvious that Nic was a great candidate to become the band's third member. After an impromptu audition in the toilet of a restaurant, the decision was made — Nic became All Saint number three.

But while the chemistry of the trio meant that their music and sound were flourishing, times were still pretty hard.

'My mum used to phone me from America all the time because she was so worried that I wasn't eating,' Nic recalled to *Top Of The Pops* magazine. 'In the beginning, when it was just Shaznay, Mel and me, we had nothing at all. We'd have to share Pot Noodles for dinner.'

Someone else who was concerned about Nic's eating habits was her big sister, Natalie, who was showing deep interest in the band's work. Ever the organiser, Nat was looking out for her kid sis and her mates, so much so that, at one point, it even looked like she might become their manager.

'I was just watching what the girls were doing and I was really interested and concerned for them,' she explains. 'I'd see what people were telling them to do and I'd be like, "No! That's not what they should be doing." I always thought I knew better!'

(Her management nous continued to operate even after she'd joined the band: 'I used to be very involved in the business side, only because I wanted us to be safe and secure, which is very important to me. Now lawyers and managers come in handy ... but it freaks me out if I think something's going on and I don't know about it. I like to be in control.')

Nat was spending a huge proportion of her time with the girls, in her role as 'band big sister', when it occurred to all four of them that she might just be the added X-factor they were looking for.

'When I first met Shaz I thought she was very shy. We went to a bar and I made her drink tequilla until she was ill, and then she became a laugh. She was really shy when I met her and she has changed a bit now. She speaks her mind now.'
*Nat*

Shaznay had been crafting a lot of her songs for four voices anyway so why not take Nat on board? Obviously she could sing — they knew this from her Catskill hotel days — and since she got on so well with the girls anyway it was a natural progression for her to join the group.

As Shaznay says, 'So many of our songs are based around four-part harmonies that when Natalie joined it was like the missing part of the puzzle!'

And so the final All Saints line-up was confirmed.

Now the girls were in full swing. It was happening. The feeling was right, the friendship was deep, and within a couple of months they'd written and recorded a whole set of demo songs.

It was time to go to the labels again...

# SIGNED, SEALED... DELIVER!

**T**hings were beginning to look rosy for the All Saints girls.

With Nic and Nat now completely settled into the band, the demos were coming out thick and fast. Shaznay's songs and the girls' love of hip-hop, combined with their solid vocals, was drawing a very original sound out of the Saints. It had 'London' stamped all over it.

It was a sound which, said Shaznay, 'was just us trying to come up with something on our own.'

Very aware that most of the singles in the charts were, as Shaznay states, 'one amazing single, with another ten trying to copy it', All Saints were determined to find their niche — a sound which was theirs and theirs alone — but a sound that could take them through a whole spectrum of musical styles.

'We never tried to be a straight R&B band, 'Shaznay later told Melody Maker journalist Taylor Parkes, '...because whenever British groups try to be a straight R&B band it just comes out crap...we're honest. And a bit more original.'

Now, armed with amazing demos and officially named All Saints after their studio location (although they did toy with the name 'Shifty'!) the girls were in first class form and ready to take on the music world.

The girls were now beginning to look like a proper outfit, which was all very peachy, but they still hadn't addressed the major question: how were they going to get a record contract? Looking back, it's ridiculous that four talented artists with such a fresh sound would have problems scoring a deal but, bizarrely, the girls were encountering two major problems when it came to signing — and, oddly, both were to do with sex!

'We found it really hard to get a record deal,'Shaznay explains. 'At first they weren't interested in us because we weren't a boy band. It was all boy bands this and boy bands that...'

Since the advent of Take That, record companies had jumped onto the boy pop wagon determined to get a piece of the puppy-love profit. Nigel Martin-Smith's ground-breaking boy band had set the world on fire — the TT lads had become the hugest pop sensation this decade, raking in the dollars from Europe and the Far East, not just through record and concert sales, but from the marketing that came with it: books, dolls, t-shirts, pillows, watches, stickers, key-fobs, pencil cases...it seemed like there wasn't an item around that didn't have a Take That logo upon it. It was brilliant managment and completely inspired marketing (Fair play to them. After all, the music business is just that — a business) and most record company moguls didn't see why they should break with a winning formula.

To them it was obvious: there were girls out there with money to spend on boy bands. And so the rush to sign up musical boy babes began.

Boyzone, OTT, Code Red, 911... the charts were suddenly full of lads doing dance routines. Short of having sex ops it didn't look like All Saints had a hope in hell of getting a record contract — any record contract, never mind one that actually let them be who they wanted to be.

Then, of course, came an added problem with a most unexpected turn of events: Spice Mania hit the mainland.

Virgin records had bravely decided to test the waters with a girl band called The Spice Girls — bravely, that is, except that, to give them credit, Geri Halliwell, Emma Bunton, Victoria Adams, Melanie Brown and Mel Chisholm had the spunk,

'I remember signing to London very well because Shaznay and I were both ill — we had flu. We were all sitting in this room with the people from the record company, signing contracts and things, and Shaz and I were snuffling into tissues. We were surrounded by snotrags. There was champagne as well and we couldn't touch it because we were both on antibiotics — so Mel and Nat guzzled away while we felt sorry for ourselves! But we were happy too. Obviously!'
*Nic*

guts and energy it took to beat the boy bands at their own game. The girls' style, energy and attitude may have been planets apart — the antithesis even — of what All Saints were trying to achieve, but with their Girl Power slogan and in-yer-face charisma was putting girl bands back in the spotlight.

It was the best of times, it was the worst of times...

'There was absolutely no interest in us...and then, then 'Wannabee'came out and they couldn't get enough of us,' says Shaznay. 'But they wanted us to be Spice...'

So many labels wanted girl bands that were an exact replica of The Spice Girls; the same image, music and attitude. All Saints wanted no part of that game. As Shaznay said later, in a band press release...

'We were determined to wait until a label was interested in us for our music and wouldn't want to change us. In our opinion that's real girl power.'

The Spice Girls thing was getting tiresome. All Saints had been penalised for being girls when the boy band scene was huge and now they were being penalised for being girls who didn't want to be the

Spicers. It was a case of 'all power to Geri and her crew' but All Saints could not and would not step into their shoes.

As Mel politely explained in an early interview with *Bliss* magazine: 'We've only got one thing in common with the Spice Girls.'Pause. 'Boobs!'

It was tough indeed. There were discussions, meetings and flirtations with record companies but all came to no avail. And then, in the middle of '96, things pretty much hit an all time low, as Mel explains.

'We've been through so much that we should have quit ages ago. The lowest point was in the middle of that year when we thought we'd just got ourselves sorted, just to be told — we want you to be like the Spice Girls.'

Hadn't they made themselves clear? She shrugs, disgustedly, shaking her head.

'"Er NO!" we said. We had to go into hiding a bit. And that was hard.'

The girls were still missing that all-important contract.

Enter John Benson.

For years Benson had been a man about town, well known in music industry circles for his efforts at sniffing out new talent. He was a highly respected man and, as luck would have it, he came into contact with the girls through Natalie.

He picks up the story:

'Natalie was a friend of mine, and in passing she'd told me about a band that her sister, Nicky, was working with. She was quite enthusiastic about it at the time and I was interested in hearing their stuff; at that point I remember, the band had been showcasing for Sony Records, which, in the end, didn't quite work out.

'Anyway, I asked Natalie for a tape but she never quite got around to it and I was working on other projects at the time. Then, I think six months later, I phoned her and Nat finally got me the tape.

'Once I'd heard it I realised that the girls could go somewhere — I could see how this could work. I met up with the band and told them that, because of my contacts and the work I had already done, I could definitely get them a good deal with a record company — and quickly.

London had seen the company go great guns with Britain's first really successful all-girl group, Banarama.

As it happens, Bennet was not over-keen to hear the All Saints tracks.

'You know how it is when a friend says "I've got something you might be interested in", Bennet told *Music Week*.

'I was a bit reluctant to hear it. But when I did put it on I realised John had brought me the best demo tape in the whole world. There were six songs on there and there were two definite potential hits.'

Bennet listened, entranced. By the time the demo had reached the first chorus in the song 'Never Ever' (which he recognised instantly to have huge hit potential) he was getting everyone in his office to hear it.

'I couldn't believe my luck,'he said. 'I've dealt with a lot of bands but Shaznay is the best writer I've ever worked with.'

Benson was also delighted.

'The other labels were also interested in signing but the girls wanted to go with London because they knew London had respect, they were cool,'he affirms. 'On top of which, London were the hungriest for the deal and I felt they had the best "machinery", with regards to the set up of the record company. We went with it.'

At last. All Saints had encountered a record company that were prepared to take them on for their music — an odd concept, sure, but one the girls, and Benson, thought could work!

And so, on December 6th '96, less than four months after meeting Benson, the girls from The Grove signed on the dotted line. The hard work was just about to start!

The girls agreed and Benson set to work, courting friends and associates at four or five of the major labels.

'Because of my contacts I was lucky in that I didn't have to take the girls through A&R departments,'he explains.

'I met the girls in the September of '96, and by October we had four or five major labels interested in the band. Eventually I saw Tracy Bennet, the head of London Records, who is a good friend of mine...'

Bennet, London's Chairman, had already been responsible for signing groups such as East Seventeen and Fine Young Cannibals to his label, and his twenty year tenure at

'I used to cry myself to sleep sometimes, it was awful. At one point I was just going to head off to France and not come back — I'd had enough. But I stuck it out because I knew we had something special. The reason we broke through out of all the girl bands is that what we are doing is substantial.'
*Mel*

# THEY KNOW WHERE IT'S AT....

From the very first words, on the very first press release, London Records proved that they knew just what All Saints were about ... and what they were about to become: 'Not just another set of wannabes,' it began. 'All Saints are four totally sussed girls into funky R&B, their self-penned debut release will be the infectious "I Know Where It's At" in the shops 18/9/97.'

It continued: 'Currently previewing their album (it's 90% complete as we speak) to ecstatic audiences in Japan, the girls will be back in the UK at the end of July to start extensive UK promotions. Next month they will be all over the press...'

London Records were taking the girls seriously. It was obvious that the bosses at the Chancellors Road headquarters were determined to get the girls the success they deserved, and that it was going to involve careful publicity and marketing strategy if they were to avoid getting the girls caught up in the Spice Girls' bandwagon. They were listening to the girls, letting them develop their music the way they wanted to, and carefully introducing them to their potential audience.

Things had been progressing smartly.

All Saints were on a learning curve. They'd already met their public, firstly on the Radio One roadshow and then doing various commercial radio concerts. Finally, as the press release revealed, they'd tucked Japan under their belts, previewing songs to Japanese audiences from their forthcoming album. It was the wildest experience.

'Visiting Japan was the best,' Shaznay recalls. 'Me and Mel had talked about going there for years. We'd kind of joked "if it all goes wrong, let's join the Japanese circus".'

It didn't look like that was going to be an option! On tour the All Saints gigs were going down a storm — audiences genuinely seemed to be reacting to their sound and style — and so the girls' confidence was soaring. Now they just needed The Hit.

As London Chairman Tracy Bennet had said, the girls' demo already had two potential hits on it, and there were plenty more where they came from. With All Saints, it wasn't going to be a case of writing and recording new material to find their first hit, it was mainly a case of recording and polishing their existing material — and then deciding what to release.

Almost as soon as the girls had signed to London, they'd got down to the business of recording. They began to work with renowned producers: Cameron McVey (Neneh Cherry's husband), who had been praised for his work with Massive Attack; K Gee of the Steve Jervier stable; and Johnny Douglas, whose name-checks included George Michael.

Everything was going pretty nicely, thank you. London were determined that the girls weren't going to be a flash in the pan — so the deal was this: they'd take an unflashy launch into the public eye and then hit 'em with the second single, 'Never Ever', which they knew would be a huge hit. The first single, it was decided, was going to be 'I Know Where It's At', a funky R&B pop tune with a slightly harder edge than anything else floating around in the charts at that time.

It was time to stoke up the press profile. The record company were back with their tiresome

'I never thought I'd be doing so much — not just performing but promotion and travel. I remember Mel and I sat up in my bed once, just after we split from ZTT, and we didn't know what was going to happen or what we were going to do. We were lying on my bed going, "Maybe we should get a deal in Japan and come out there first." Then what happens? We get a deal and one of the first countries we go to happens to be Japan! Just shows, you've got to take each day as it comes.'

*Shaznay*

'Seeing us, All Saints, on television never struck me so much as the first time it happened, which was when the video for "I Know Where It's At" was shown. Someone at the record company had told me we were going to be on MTV so I remember being at home with my mum waiting for it to come on. It was, like, ages and ages before it came on – all these other tunes were playing and then, just when we weren't expecting it, it came on. We were yelling and shouting and screaming ... jumping up and down. And then just glued to the telly – even though I'd obviously seen it before it was just weird that it was going into people's homes and bars and stuff. It was weird. Now, actually, I don't get that freaked out any more at seeing myself on TV because it's ... well ... I just don't think of the other people who see it. I think I feel like it's only me looking at it. I just felt weird that first time.'

*Shaznay*

problem: With all the Spice wannabes around, how were they going to market All Saints without being caught up in the teen-pop sensation? They needed to get coverage in the credible media. As it happened, the music spoke for itself.

The press team at London Records sent out six-track demos to the music press and waited for a reaction. It was atomic. *The Face*, never a magazine to take its music lightly, decided to run an entire spread on the girls, just on the merits of the demo. It was All Saints' first chance to speak to the record-buying public, and they made their message clear.

'We're not pushovers,' they said. 'People see four young girls and think they can manipulate us. We've tried to keep the music as real as possible.'

*The Face* were impressed, and Craig McClean, who wrote the piece, summed up their reaction in his final sentence: 'They're All Saints,' he wrote. 'And they're all right by us.'

They were all right by a lot of the other 'grown-up' magazine titles, too. *Sky* magazine was equally impressed by the six-track, and ran an eight-page feature on the girls. And when they met them they were as impressed by their personalities as by their music: it was obvious that All Saints were much, much more than a group of girls jumping on to the sudden girl-band wagon.

'It was obvious from the outset that All Saints were artists we'd be interested in,' says *Sky*'s Assistant Editor, Sophie Wilson. 'The first time I came across them was when we got the promo video from the record company. It made a real impact. Not only did they look amazing but the music was excellent. They just seemed so much less manufactured than a lot of bands around at the time.

'They were, are, just right for *Sky*. They're sexy but real too, laid-back. You get the feeling you could hang out with them. And that, with the combination of their music, which is definitely credible, works.' She laughs. 'They, er, know where it's at!'

As the date of the single release neared, press interest began to soar. Now the teen mags were getting keen — *TV Hits*, *Smash Hits*, *Top Of The Pops* and *Bliss* all carried interviews with the girls — and television producers were equally interested. *The Big Breakfast* lined the girls up to do an early morning preview of their single, launching a long-term love affair the show has had with them ever since. And then came the biggy: *The National Lottery Draw*, with one of the largest audiences a band could hope for, wanted them to perform on the very day of the planned single release. It was happening...

The girls were also beginning to get their first taste of fame. People were beginning to recognise them in the street, much to Shaznay's horror.

'The first time we did TV, for the National Lottery, my family told me that after the show had ended all the neighbours on our street came out of their houses and pointed to her bedroom window, going "That's where she sleeps",' Shaznay revealed later to *FHM*. 'That's just a bit too off-key.'

In London, the buzz was beginning to reach fever pitch. Questions were being asked: Did anybody know anything about these girls? What was the score? Weren't they the girls from Ladbroke Grove they'd seen at so and so?

Bit by bit the questions started to get answered as the London Records press office's prediction — that the girls would be all over the press — became true.

Then tragedy struck. Just days into the scheduled release of 'I Know Where It's At', it was announced that the Princess of Wales had died in an appalling car accident in Paris. The nation was plunged into mourning. No one felt like celebrating anything. The release of a debut single certainly seemed inconsequential.

Shaznay, possibly at one of the most emotionally mixed times in her life, wrote 'War of Nerves', the last song to be added to the All Saints' album. 'Everybody suddenly got scared because it was such a shock,' she told record company bosses for a band press release. 'It brought the subject of death closer to a lot of people who hadn't experienced it.'

Apart from the obvious despair brought on by the news and the weeks of mourning, the death of the Princess had a further effect on the music industry. Most radio stations, who would have been playing the month's new releases, had forfeited all up-tempo songs for sadder, calmer songs reflecting the mood of the nation. As callous as it sounds, it could have been disastrous for All Saints.

But while record company executives dining in city restaurants could be heard to complain about the effect the tragedy had had on their latest releases, the reply that kept coming back was always the same: 'Yeah. You can say so and so has suffered because of the airplay situation. But then why have All Saints charted so well?'

Because they had.

All Saints had done it. Against all odds, the girls had managed to sell enough copies of their debut single to get them into the charts. If the publicity surrounding the girls had been mad before, it was madder now: interest in the girls was self-generating and suddenly every magazine, TV show and pop compilation CD was looking for a piece of All Saints to add a bit of credibility.

The record kept on selling, and in mid-September it peaked ... at number four.

Shaznay's schoolmate's prediction, 'see you on *Top Of The Pops*', had come true. All Saints were a hit.

# THE SAINTS GO MARCHING IN!

**W**hen All Saints found out about the success of their first single they were stuck in a hotel in Germany doing yet more promotional work.

'I couldn't believe it,' said Mel later, laughing. 'We were in Germany and were like...' (she raises her eyes to the ceiling) '...that's great! And we're still here...'

The girls were slaving their botties off. The success of 'I Know Where It's At' simply meant that more TV shows had yet more reasons to have the girls on for longer. It also meant more press interviews, more promo work — generally more travelling. By the end of September, All Saints could have done reports for Thomas Cook's.

The girls were learning about pop-star survival: suddenly sunglasses weren't just things you wore to look cool, they were things that hid the bin-bags under your eyes and jet-lag was now something that made life hell for a week after a long-haul flight — not something that gave you an excuse to stay in bed for three days. If only they had the time!

It didn't help that Shaznay and Nat realised they hated flying. ('I'm really scared of flying,' Nat smiled. 'I always think, How the hell's this big thing going to get up there? I get really tired when we're travelling and it's hard to be perfect and fresh all the time.')

The girls quickly picked up tips from the other bands out on the road. They were developing a travel plan. It seemed you needed three main things for travelling:

1) Sunglasses. 'I need my sunglasses,' said Mel. 'They cover your face. Hide the tiredness. The bigger the better!'

2) A mobile phone. As Nic said, 'I need to have some kind of communication. Actually, to be honest no one ever phones me... But I like to be in touch with my family, otherwise I just phone everybody.' Shaznay had got her little Ericsson for the same reason. 'I need my mobile so my mum can get in contact,' she smiled.

3) The final thing the girls needed for travelling was anything that would help them get sleep, like Nat's super sexy blow-it-up, shrink-it-down,

'Travelling to different countries is frustrating because we don't get to look around. In the beginning it was fun to know we were going to be going all over the world. But it's actually dissapointing because we don't get to see what's about, we're stuck in a hotel room all day. Usually it's too hard to do anything anyway and we've got lots of interviews all day. If we do a show we go outside, but not for long.'

*Shaznay*

flight pillow. 'I've got to have my blow-up pillow that goes around my neck,' she explained. 'I got my first one before we went to Japan last time. But then someone stole it. Johnny [their tour manager] bought my second one. But it's great. You need it in this job. Anything to help us get sleeeep!'

Sleep was something the girls didn't seem to have the time to do. As with any band new to the machinations of the music industry, the girls were having to adjust to the hard work involved. Not that they hadn't done hard work before — it's just that this was harder.

Most of their days were starting before 7.30.

It was a typical British band schedule: nip into Germany for a TV show and then into, say, France for a quick interview before making it home for midnight — if you're lucky. On other days they'd be zipping up and down the UK to do personal appearances and interviews. As anyone who burns the candle at both ends will tell you, eventually you crack.

Nat started to show signs of pressure at a shoot for Sky when, after about four hours of posing and preening (without one word of complaint, and consummate professionalism), the effect of the hard work made her feel woozy and she had to call time on the shoot.

But then maybe that week had been a little tougher than most — after all, the girls had been presenting The Big Breakfast! All Saints had, at this point, become so popular that the producers at Planet 24, The Big Breakfast's production company, had asked Mel, Shaznay, Nic and Nat to step into presenter Denise Van Outen's shoes (not literally, you understand) to present a week of the show's early morning slots from 27 to 31 October.

As their press office said: 'The girls were asked to present the show a few weeks ago and foolishly agreed; without realising the 4.30 a.m. call times.'

Still. The Big Breakfast was a hoot. They spent a week larking around in the early mornings (where they 'met a man who knew about spiders and a man who knew about teeth') and generally had a giggle. And by the next week, when they'd received their lovely bunches of thank-you flowers from the show's big boss, Duncan Gray, it was fair to say that All Saints were as much household names as Heinz Baked Beanz, and just as tasty.

There was a wee problem. Unfortunately Mel had unwittingly upset a couple of Big Breakfast viewers when engaged in a head to head row with an upstart from a pop group. (She used a bad word.) The Big Breakfast had to apologise to the ITC and Mel got a bit of bad rap from the press.

'In some ways that was a real low point for me,' Nicky explains now. 'I think we realised just then that we were going to have to watch our words, that we couldn't be ourselves — that we couldn't say anything we wanted. It was a bit depressing really. Like, everyone was watching us.'

Everybody was watching them. And now that everybody knew the basic facts about the girls, the teen press were laying in with their sillier questions. What item of clothing would you never wear? (Shaznay: Lycra cycling shorts.) If you had to be an animal what would it be? (Mel: a

tortoise because they don't have to do a lot, do they?) Generally the girls' patience was incredible, and suddenly they seemed to be having fun with the daftness of the situation.

Shaznay, of course, was still getting spooked out by the whole fame thang. Recognition, she admitted to journalists, was one of the best parts of the job, but she was continually freaked out when she was on stage and heard a couple of thousand girls singing her songs back to her. As she told the *NME*, she'd think: 'Hello. How do you know my song? That I wrote in my bedroom?'

October was a landmark for Shaznay, as it happens: she experienced her first 'pop-star birthday'. Coming off stage at Pepsi Pop, in Rotterdam, she was greeted by the young chaps from the pop band N-Sync who sang 'Happy Birthday' to her and presented her with a huge cake.

As journalists stood around and noted that All Saints dived into the cake with glee (these weren't some airy fairy girls who wouldn't eat cake to save calories), Shaznay also found herself denying her first public love rumour: word had it that she'd been dating one of the lads from Boys II Men.

'We've been friends for years,' she smiled like a pro. 'Nothing more than that.'

While the teen press was going a bit hoopla, luckily the tabloid press had not yet started digging the dirt. Of course the girls weren't naive, and knew it was just a matter of time before the muck-raking would start.

In a remarkable display of foresight, *Big* magazine questioned the girls about how they'd feel if their ex-boyfriends started selling their stories to the papers.

'They're pretty decent blokes,' Mel had said. 'They wouldn't do that.'

But Nat had gone, in the words of the journalist, 'slightly green'. 'I'm a little worried about that happening,' she said. 'I don't want to be embarrassed in front of my family.' Unfortunately she had the tabloid 'scandal' still to look forward to.

All in all, it had been a great few months for the Saints. They'd had a top-five single, massive TV exposure, lots of live experience and more than adequate press interest.

Here they were, at the end of October '97, hardly recognising themselves as the 'young hopefuls' they'd been at the beginning of the year. But the next month was going to be telling.

The next four weeks were going to see the girls release their second — and slightly unusual — single 'Never Ever', which would show once and for all whether the girls were going to be one-hit

wonders. Then, of course, they were all aboard the *Smash Hits* tour bus, famous for its ability to showcase future superstars, and after that, right at the end of the month, was the launch of the girls' debut album.

It was a turning point, and they all felt it.

At one point, as they huddled into London's Pineapple dance studios, waiting to begin choreography work for the new single, the girls thought about where they'd like to be by this time next year.

'I'd like to have paid off my parents' mortgage,' said Mel.

'Yeah, I'd like my mum to have stopped working,' Shaznay said.

And while Nic thought more, Nat grinned: 'I want a council flat in Hackney,' she said. 'Oh. I've already got that. No. I want a thing on my wall with two big platinum discs saying "All Saints" on them.'

'But Nat,' laughed Nic, 'we've already got ours...'

She was joking, but little did she realise that they didn't have long to wait.

'Shaz's friends always phone her whie she's away and ask where she is and she has to ask us. I've woken up at home when the phone rang next to the bed and I thought it was my wake-up call. It was just a friend. I was like, "Hello! Good morning! But it's a day off!"'

*Nicky*

# NEVER EVER SAY NEVER...

The single that was going to prove to be the making of All Saints — the single which Tracy Bennet had immediately predicted would be the stormer for the girls — was 'Never Ever', a song that couldn't be more different from the girls' first release.

Where 'I Know Where It's At' was funked up and closer to pop, the second single was unlike anything that had been in the charts for ages, and was described on its press release as 'a slinky rhythmic, laid back number whose rap can't fail to strike a chord in everyone's heart'.

Sylvia Patterson in the *NME* had other words for it: she described it as a 'modern classic ... all Shangri-las, breathy spoken bits and a sumptuous harmonic groove'. It was, she said, 'the sexiest tune of the year by man, woman or vegetable'.

'Never Ever' was — is — one of those infectious, never-forgotten songs. Once heard it will linger for hours: hear it at breakfast, hum it at lunch, sing it at tea. Unlike other similarly infectious tunes out in 1997, however, 'Never Ever' was a crafted classic — a properly written song, with a clever harmony and a gifted lyric, not just a throwaway ditty mastered for aqua-aerobics in the holiday hotel swimming pool.

Amazingly, the record very nearly didn't see the light of day. 'Never Ever' was a song she had not planned for release. 'I'm a hip-hop person,' Shaznay had shrugged, while explaining the events to her record company. 'I like up-tempo tracks

with big beats and "Never Ever" just stayed on the shelf.'

She continued: 'I wrote it when I was at rock bottom. There was a lot of hurt and it all came crashing down at the same time Mel was feeling the same way, so she could really relate to it.'

Luckily Shaznay had given a copy of the song to Nicky, who played it to her friends and family. The feedback she got was astounding, possibly because 'Never Ever' is the kind of song everyone can relate to.

What it's actually about is the end of Shaznay's first major relationship, throwing up the kind of questions we all ask when a love affair goes unfathomably wrong: What happened here? Did I do something? Have I changed? Am I going mad 'cause I thought everything was all right? In summary, what the song was saying was, 'For God's sake, tell me what's gone on here or I'll lose my mind.' Everyone had been there, done that, bought the hooded sweatshirt.

When *Vox* magazine later asked Shaznay if her ex had actually answered her questions — told her to her face, told her on the phone, or written her that letter giving her the answers — she revealed that while she'd never got the letter, he *had* phoned her up.

'I got to know some of it,' she said. 'But it's very confusing 'cause at the end of the day you still kind of blame each other...'

The video for the single was just as amazing as the record itself — and very fitting. Directed by Sean Ellis, the promo intermingled home-cine 60s-style shots of the girls happily hanging out by a pool with stark shots of a harder-edged black-clad All Saints, lamenting in the song while destruction occurred around them. The stunning dark side effects of exploding windows mixed with the scenes of sunshine and happiness summed up the feelings everyone has when involved in a separation: the happy memories curdled by feelings of utter devastation. The video certainly left a bitter aftertaste. It was brilliant.

'Making the video took two long days,' Shaznay says now. 'The flashback scenes were worst. At one point everyone got in the pool, but I didn't. It was too cold! It was shot in Tooting Bec [in London]. It was freezing! The others were diving in and out and I sat on the side!'

All Saints were unknowingly entering one of the most exciting times of their lives. As the single was released they scored up another 'first': they got the cover of *Smash Hits*.

While *Smash Hits* may be a teen mag, it is historically a prestigious milestone in any artist's career to make it to the cover. It's a stepping stone on the way to somewhere — a feat that's been carried out by every megastar from George Michael to Madonna — and as such it's a statement that a band has arrived. Even if they quickly depart again, they can truly hold their heads up and say that they made it!

On 5 November All Saints achieved the feat: *Smash Hits* hit the news-stands with their picture plastered all over it — the girls wearing devils' horns for a bit of pop irony.

'All Saints! The confessions of pop's cheekiest devils,' read the cover line. The feature inside was a bit of daftness — a test of scruples for Shaznay and co — but it was showing a side of All Saints that was becoming more prevalent: All Saints having a laugh!

One of the questions posed was this: If the man who announced the charts left his top forty list in a cafe, and All Saints came across it, would they take a sneaky peek — and maybe change their chart position — before handing it back?

'I wouldn't need to change anything,' said Nic. 'Our record would be number one anyway.'

Quite a prophecy.

The girls, of course, were a natural choice for the annual *Smash Hits* tour — the pop tour which takes in venues around the country before culminating in a national televised Poll-Winners' Party. And so it was that from 18 to 23 November the girls joined the party, alongside Peter Andre, Ant and Dec, Kavana, Five, 911, No Mercy and N Sync. The six-date tour took in Bournemouth, Cardiff, Manchester, Sheffield, Newcastle and Birmingham — for the girls it was yet another opportunity for them to experience arena performing.

The Poll-Winners' Party, televised at the end of the tour, saw All Saints taking to the stage beside the likes of Janet Jackson (Shaznay sporting her new longer locks for the event!) and, while they may not have carried off an award, they did make it to runners-up in the Best New Act of 97 category. And they hadn't been known for that long when the voting took place!

Meanwhile the single was turning out to be a proper hit — a slower grower, picking up momentum, more fans and more sales as the weeks went on.

'If "Never Ever" had gone straight in at number one, I'd have thought it was just the kids who bought "I Know Where It's At" buying it. But it took time to get there. This means it wasn't just bought by the people who were thinking about the way we looked or something. It was people who heard it over and over until it grew on them and they went out and bought it.'

*Shaznay*

'I personally always thought "Never Ever" was a number-one track. A lot of people really relate to "Never Ever": a woman came up to me and said how she could totally understand where it was coming from. People like to be able to relate to songs, especially if they're in that situation.'

*Nicky*

'Never Ever' had already become an anthem. Schoolyards were full of young girls chanting Nicky's intro ('A few questions that I have to know...') and every radio station seemed to be churning the song out on an A-list. It was on *Eastenders*, it was on *Corrie*, it was playing at the local ice-rink...

('It's driving me mad,' a journalist told the girls. 'Every time I go into the office kitchen someone's humming it.' There were looks of sympathy all round...)

While the single sold in its thousands, All Saints' personal popularity seemed to be growing too. Men's mags were quoting them as this year's most-fanciables. Television shows were chasing them for interviews (Natalie displayed a nifty talent for computer games when she thrashed her three mates on *Gamesmaster*!) and the girls were generally picking up fans in the teen press.

*TV Hits* reported that at a recent mag shoot the girls had been mobbed by local kids who spotted them posing near their houses. Instead of throwing pop-star strops, or showing disdain, the Saints had invited the kids to join in with the pictures and walked around with them afterwards. The staff at the mag were impressed.

Unfortunately another medium was beginning to show interest in Nicky, Nat, Mel and Shaznay. It had to happen and it did: the tabloids wanted their piece of All Saints and they were hell-bent on getting it. The girls were beginning to suffer for their fame...

'Nat hurt her leg when shooting the video for "Never Ever". As she walks past the camera a window explodes behind her. She looks pained if you watch closely.'

*Mel*

'It was awful! I had burns up my leg. They could only shoot one take – "Don't worry, it won't hurt," they said. I'm sure it wouldn't have hurt if I was wearing thicker trousers or the trousers that stunt people wear. But they were thin Armani trousers and it felt like I was being stung the whole time, and afterwards I looked at my leg and there were red blood circles all down it. When you see the video, the look on my face is total pain. I'm smiling but gritting my teeth.'

*Nat*

# WAIT TILL YOU HEAR THE ALBUM...

In the typical build 'em up and knock 'em down tradition of the British tabloids, the UK newspapers had finally clicked onto All Saints and were digging for dirt with mechanical shovels. Shaznay, Nic, Nat and Mel were a tabloid hack's dream: four stunning girls in their early twenties, who were talented, sexy and had attitude. When 'Never Ever' brought the Saints to their attention, the tabloids must have thought all their Christmases had come at once.

Everyone in the All Saints camp knew it was just a matter of time before journos started looking for scandal, and it turned out that the festive season was when it was going to happen. Merry Christmas, girls.

The focus of the press corps turned out to be the Appleton sisters, the first story to rear its head being about Nat. As it turned out, it was the non-story about Nat having a daughter and being married — the first point being true, the second being complete rubbish. As Nat stated earlier, the marriage had been annulled.

Hot on the heels of that little 'nugget-of-news' was a story about Nicky, and how she'd moved to Manchester at one point to live with her 'fiancé',

who happened to be a brother of Nat's boyfriend of the time. Scorching stuff. As it happens, if anyone had bothered to check, Nic had actually told the story herself to *Top Of The Pops* magazine in August.

'Nat set me up with the brother of her boyfriend,' she said. 'Two days later I moved from London to Manchester to live with him ... my mother still chucks a wobbly when I mention his name!' It was now December and the story had first appeared in August. That's how much of an exclusive it was.

So that was the way it was going to be from now on. Nat and the girls were going to be referred to as 'All Saints Stunnas' and every piece of their history, no matter how inconsequential, would be dragged up for public titillation. Ow.

Nic and Nat dismissed the stories. Why should they care? They soon realised that the old adage of 'today's news, tomorrow's fish and chip wrappers' was entirely true and, anyway, both of them were achieving something with their lives — something which didn't involve hurting other people, unlike the lads who had sold their stories.

'Make your money, you losers,' Nat smiled. As far as she was concerned, she and her sister had done nothing wrong, and cashing in on someone was the lowest thing a man could do.

Shaznay was disgusted. She admitted to magazine journalists that she wasn't going out

'K Gee is like a brother to us. He's been there from the very beginning. He worked with us on "I Know Where It's At" before we even signed to London so it's kind of nice that that's the first track we put out and the first one to chart. He's part of our team, K Gee. He comes up with the most amazing backing tracks and then we all collaborate until we've got a song. For instance, he might write a backing track and then, in the studio, he'll see who's vibing off it the most. That person will take it home, write the vocal track and then we'll get together and learn it.'

*Shaznay*

because of the tabloid coverage. As she pointed out, at least a tenth of the population had had the stuff happen to them that had been reported about Nat and Nic in the tabloids. Putting it in the papers, she said, was 'just nasty'.

Still, the girls had something positive to concentrate on. 'Never Ever' was still riding high and, on 24 November, they'd released their album, *All Saints*.

The reviews had been stonking. 'On the strength of this album, All Saints are bound for somewhere near the top,' said *The Times*. 'Shows much sassy promise,' said *Big Issue*. And so it went on...

'We wrote our whole album ourselves, so it's heartfelt. There's some truth to it,' Shaznay reflects now. 'We've tried to cover all areas, so it's mellow ... All of us listen to rap, and there's a lot of funk in the album. Its not a straight-out pop album. Every band has its own niche, but I think our niches isn't forced on us, it isn't fake. There's no one telling us how to act, sing or what to write. It's what we want to do. That was reflected in the album.'

The album shocked a lot of people who had clapped eyes on the girls, seen a bevy of beauties and not really taken that much notice of the tunes they were emitting. It was the kind of record a serious music collector could not be without. Alongside the first two singles, 'I Know Where It's At' and, of course, 'Never Ever', were a couple of brilliantly executed covers (Labelle's 70s smash 'Lady Marmalade', Red Hot Chilli Peppers' 'Under The Bridge', done because 'it was the last thing people expected us to do' which made up the double-A-side third single) and a few self-penned masterpieces — 'Booticall', 'Heaven' and 'Beg'.

'Oh maaan! What can I say?' laughed Shaznay when asked about the steamy lyric in 'Booticall'. She stopped for a giggle. 'It's about those blokes who phone you at 1.00 a.m. and ask you to come around to get down. It's our take on that situation. It's just a booticall. It's funny!'

'Ha, that's nothing,' Nic laughed. 'You should hear "Get Busy"!'

> 'Shaznay has that All Saints sound, what we want and where we want to be. Her writing is very strong.'
> Mel

Again, Shaznay laughed off the song lyric. '"Get Busy"? Ha. Er, well. Yeah, that's what it is. It's about when you've just started dating someone and you're not sure what to do because you don't know what the other person's like. But you know what? To me it's funny because it's so explicit ... and it rhymes!'

'Get Busy' didn't actually make it to the album. One song that did, 'Beg', had absolutely no sexual undertones. What it was, explained Shaznay, was, 'a message to people in the industry who didn't want to know us when we were struggling and then they wanted to be best mates with us when we got our deal. They know who they are.'

This was it; finally the girls had something real to hold up and wave at their detractors. Throughout the years of slaving, amid the disappointments, in between fights, all the girls had ever wanted was to get an album of their songs on sale — to get their stuff heard. And here it was.

As the CD sold by the rack-full, All Saints were suddenly everywhere. There were few music lovers who weren't sporting a copy of the album, with its dark, sophisticated portrait of Nic, Nat, Mel and Shaznay. Oddly, the cover, amazing as it was, was the one thing that the girls weren't ecstatic about. Nic reckoned that they originally wanted to photocopy parts of their bodies (legs, arms, Shaznay's teeth when she was wearing her brace) and paste the bits together for a pastiche cover. 'I don't think we pushed it enough!' said Nic.

Of course, the truth of the matter was that the girls' looks *were* going to help the album sell. While the way they looked wasn't going to earn All Saints their credibility, it might help a few people to discover their sound — a few people who otherwise might not have ventured into All Saints territory.

'There's no getting around that,' Nat told *Loaded*. 'That's the way it is in pop. At least for women. There's definitely a requirement for girls in bands to be sexy. But we're not interested in playing up to that.'

They really didn't need to. With the album enjoying such a great reception, All Saints launched into December on a high. The first week of the month saw them performing at the Concert of Hope for the Diana, Princess of Wales, Memorial Fund. In a makeshift 6,000-capacity indoor arena, next to Battersea power station, the girls gave it their all, alongside Robbie Williams, Damage, Peter Andre, Boyzone, 911 and Gary Barlow.

As ever, All Saints were making critics stand up and take notice. The man from *The Times* was intrigued. 'Signs of a powerful quartet in the making,' he wrote in his report.

All this time 'Never Ever' had still been 'shifting units' in the charts and, by mid-December, it was riding high in the top five. However, the betting-shop punters who were laying their money on All Saints making it to a Christmas number one were a tad disappointed. They didn't make the slot.

But all things come to those who wait. As the year turned the girls were in for a well-deserved surprise. Having appeared on *Top Of The Pops* virtually every week since the single's release, 'Never Ever' eventually made it to the top spot.

All Saints had their first number one.

As it happened, the girls had made music industry history. 'Never Ever' had sold more records before reaching number one (770,000, in fact) than any single in chart history. It actually sold more copies when it was at number two than it did a week later at number one.

What the industry was looking at here, then, was a classic single, a record for all time, one that would still be on radio playlists ten or twenty years from now. Shaznay had obviously written a corker. It was a great way to start 1998.

On 31 December 1997 a new issue of *Mizz* magazine went on sale, carrying a brief interview with the Saints. 'Why was 1998 going to be great for All Saints?' asked the mag.

'Because of all the hard work we've put into the group,' said Mel. 'The shows, the album, the single. Everything we did in '97 was geared towards this year.'

What a year it was going to be, mate...

'Apart from "Never Ever" being a classic, I think "Take The Key" and "Alone" are the best songs on the album. With "Alone", I got the backing track from K Gee and I wrote it. It's one of the tracks that turned out exactly as I wanted it to sound – the verses sounding like someone's on the phone. I love "Take The Key". It's a nice love song. "Beg"'s cool actually but it's one of the songs I had the most problems with. With all the songs I've ever written, it's like you write and record it and "boom" it's there. With "Beg" I had to go and change some of the lyrics because they didn't turn out right. My manager pointed out a few things to me, like, I've got this habit: I will write too many words to sing. I can fit them in when I sing but not everyone else in the group can! With "Beg" I cut out a few words, changed a few around ... it had loads of melodies going down and I had to cut them back a bit. It's cool though. I'm happy with it.'

Shaznay

# THE BRITS!

**M**onday 9 February, 1998. London's Docklands Arena: the date and venue of the British music industry's most important shindig of the year: the Brits. Wrapped around tables, crammed into the auditorium of the LDA, the country's assembled music moguls and attending media were waiting to find out the names of the artists and producers who were to be honoured by the industry this year.

All Saints were hot tips.

The press had already placed their bets. They were predicting at least one gong for the London Records signing but, as is always the case at these events, no one was sure. Some of the tabloids were already billing the event as a battle of girl bands, the Saints versus the Spices. It was the last thing on the girls' minds.

All Saints had been selected to perform at the event, which was a huge honour in itself, and had spent the morning rehearsing for the gig. The girls were to perform with the East London Gospel Choir, and those lucky enough to catch a glimpse at rehearsals had been awestruck. It was an event not to be missed.

The host for the evening was author/comedian Ben Elton (an old hand at the job — this was his second time) and as he set to with the proceedings his enthusiasm was evident. He was, as he said, a music fan, and tonight he was standing on a stage watching some of the most talented artists perform — a multitude of gigs in one night. He was ecstatic.

Less than twenty minutes into proceedings, All Saints were 'up'. They were the second act to perform on the show — and what an act! Introducing them as 'the awesome foursome', Elton grinned knowledgeably as he turned to the stage to watch All Saints do their stuff for the ladies and gentlemen of the music industry.

Flanked on either side by pyramids of parka-clad choir members, the girls launched into possibly the most amazing set of the evening. The song was, of course, 'Never Ever' (*still* in the charts after all this time). As it began a couple of the girls' die-hard fans were at the front of the stage giving their support: 'Go, Shaznay!'

Shaznay grinned at the fans as Mel eased herself into the song: 'My head's spinning...'

It was tight, it was stunning. It couldn't have been more different from the Spice Girls' fantastic spot, later. The girls had done what they'd set out to achieve — *all* they'd wanted to achieve — which was to get *their* music heard on *their* terms.

> 'I remember being so scared about performing. I was the first one up as well — I had to do the beginning bit of the song ("a few questions that I need to know") and I was shaking so hard. I thought I'd forget the words. It was just the enormity of the whole situation.'
> *Nicky*

The song came to an end with a special solo vocal spot from Shaznay, met with rapturous applause from the audience. 'Well,' said a stunned Ben Elton. 'What about that! You do not mess with that!'

And you didn't. It was fantastic. A year ago no one at the Brits had even heard of All Saints and then here they were stunning the audience with their first-ever ceremony performance.

Now the gossip in the auditorium was rife: with an act like that All Saints must have won something. But what? They didn't have long to find out.

It was time for the nominees to be announced for the best video award. The 'Never Ever' video flashed up on the screen and a hoot went up at the Docklands Arena. The video was fantastic. It had to have won, hadn't it?

Hadn't it?

Thirty seconds later we heard the answer: It had.

The camera panned in on the All Saints table. The girls were beside themselves with excitement. Natalie had already jumped to her feet, victoriously, mouthing to the camera in front of her,

'Yes! Yes!' She stormed up onto the stage, the others following seconds later.

Shaznay had the giggles. 'Look! We did it!' she shouted, as she held up the statue of Britannia. The rest of the girls were speechless. Then there were thanks for the video director. 'Sean Ellis, I love you!' shouted Shaznay. The other girls piped in with their own words of appreciation.

And then, as quickly as it had begun, it was over. The girls were climbing down from the stage.

They were stunned. There had been times when All Saints had wondered if they'd ever get a decent record out, never mind an award for it. And now, here they were in February 1998, with a number-one single under their belt, a platinum-selling album and a Brit Award to stick on their mantelpiece.

How could it possibly get any better?

Of course they knew it could. The girls had also been nominated for Best Single, an award that would probably mean more to them than most because it was about their music and only their music. And of course, to Shaznay, getting the award would seem like a miracle. She wrote the single at one of the unhappiest times of her life — could it possibly lead her to one of her happiest?

Ben Elton introduced the celebrities who were going to announce the award — down the stairs came Hollywood superstars Samuel L. Jackson and Pam Grier, in Britain to publicise their new Quentin Tarantino film *Jackie Brown*.

'What's up?' shouted Samuel as he neared the podium.

'The nominees for Best Single are...'

The videos flashed up on the large screens. Once again, there were shots from 'Never Ever' and, once again, screams went up in the Docklands Arena.

'And the winner is ... All Saints.'

They'd done the double. The girls were walking away from their first Brits ceremony with two awards. It was unbelievable.

The view as the cameras panned onto the All Saints table this time was very different from half an hour before. This time there were tears. Natalie and Nic were hugging each other crying. Mel and Shaznay were gripping each other incredulously.

'I still can't believe I cried during the second speech! I'm so ashamed! I can't even watch the rerun now. A few months later we had to do this record company reception in Germany and they had a huge screen up showing the bit where we won the Best Single award with me crying all over the place. The other girls were getting tearful but I was just standing there with my eyes closed, my hands on my ears ... I just can't look at it. I look so ugly apart from anything else!'

*Shaznay*

Just a quick flick back to two years before would have seen them in very different circumstances.

When the girls eventually made it to the stage (mascara tear stains visible on Nat's face) the auditorium grew silent as Shaznay stood in front of the microphone.

'I'm so embarrassed,' she laughed, stifling her sobs. 'Thank you to everyone.' She was having trouble holding back the tears now. 'It's funny,' she said, 'how something so good can click from such a bad situation.'

Everyone knew what she was talking about. When she'd written 'Never Ever' she was heartbroken and her musical career was floundering. Look at her now...

She paused. 'Nuff respect,' she said, 'to anyone who gets up in the morning and knows what they want to do with their lives.'

As they began to walk away from the microphone Mel chipped in.

'Thanks to all our mothers!' she grinned.

The girls returned to their seats shell-shocked; Ben Elton looked on grinning. It was good to see an award go to girls who had worked so hard for it.

The celebrations went on into the night. The girls partied big time at the after-show party where, backstage, TV show *The O Zone* caught them in their award-winning afterglow. Are you happy? they asked.

'Very happy,' said Nic, smiling at Mel.

Were those tears that we'd seen on stage?

'Yeah,' laughed Nic. 'Actually no. It was an illusion!'

'Yeah,' butted in Mel. 'It was like special effects.' She grinned wickedly at the presenter. 'Our mums are here,' she explained, 'so it's making the tears come more.'

They were determined to

have a fantastic end to an amazing evening.

The next day, as the debris was being cleared from the London Docklands Arena, the front pages of the papers were plastered with pictures of Shaznay, Mel, Nic and Nat, telling the story of how All Saints had won two Brits under their own steam — singing their own songs their own way without any record company manipulation or manager manufacturing. The conclusion was that, unlike a lot of those around today, All Saints were a group, not a business.

Of course, the girls had realised by now that they couldn't escape the tabloid gossip-mongering that was surrounding their private lives. The words appearing under the *Daily Star* masthead today were 'Ooooh, aaah ... Saints 'n' winnaaaahs', and on the front page, under the headline 'Heaven For Saint Nicky', was a story claiming that 'All Saints stunner Nicky Appleton' had been publicly confirmed as the new love in Robbie Williams' life.

And as the story spilled onto page three ('Nicky Drives Robbie Bananas' — cue picture of Robbie eating a banana!) the real story we were looking for was on page two: the tale of how All Saints had stolen the show and had eventually reaped the fruits of all of their hard work. The headline said it all:

'SAINTS MARCH IN!'

# SOMETHING LIKE A PHENOMENON

'It has been a weird time. Quite tiring. But it's been good to see everything that we've worked for actually happen.'

It's almost half a year now since All Saints picked up their Brits gongs and Shaznay Lewis is, as per usual, trying to cram her life into the two days she'll have free for the next six weeks.

As she speaks there are strange, watery noises emanating from her side of the phone.

'Sorry about the noise. I'm having a bath!'

Shaznay's becoming a bit of an expert at doing two things at once.

Today all the Saints are frantically trying to fit in their chores ... Natalie is with her daughter trying to get her 'ordinary' life in order before the next take-off; Nick is in the studio with her boyfriend, Robbie Williams; a blossoming Mel is moving house and Shaznay is having a splash about ('I spent yesterday in the studio. It's mad even when we're at home. Not complaining though...')

It hasn't calmed down for All Saints, you see. The Brits success is not the climax of the All Saints story — it is, as Shaznay insists, an ongoing epic.

Ever since that February night at Docklands, the girls have continued to make headline news as their celebrity ('the thing we actually dislike the most' — Mel) reaches mammoth proportions.

Take a look at their diaries and you get the sense of a schedule that has accelerated to exhausting levels. A typical few weeks early in the year looked like this: 21 February: *Top of The Pops*; 25-27 February: promotion in France, Spain and Germany; 28 February: sign three-album publishing deal with MCA; 5 March: Germany's Echo Awards; March 10: Miami ...

And so it goes on.

Within months of receiving their Brits gongs, All Saints had managed to put another stamp on the charts, releasing their inspired cover versions of 'Under The Bridge' and 'Lady Marmalade' as a double-A-sided single. Hand in hand with the songs came a spectacular video — a £500,000 mini-movie using stunts masterminded by the *Batman and Robin* special effects team. The vid was shown in cinema screenings of Quentin Tarantino's film *Jackie Brown*, in a bid to raise cash for the breast cancer charity Breakthrough ('Breakthrough was something we'd already been involved in so it seemed like a good idea,' — Mel). Cue more newspaper headlines.

Fast forward two months. It's now the weekend of 16 May and All Saints have been invited to perform at the Symphony Hall in Birmingham for the G8 summit. Performing in front of the world's most powerful leaders — German Chancellor Helmut Kohl; Japanese Prime Minister Ryutaro Hashimoto; Prime Minister Tony Blair; US President Bill Clinton — the girls do their stuff, finishing with a rendition of the Beatles classic 'All You Need Is Love'.

By Monday all the newspapers — tabloid and broadsheet — are carrying a picture of the girls chatting with Bill Clinton. Get that: a picture of them and the most powerful man in the world. Now that's what I call famous!

Oddly, the girls don't have an adequate grasp of how big they really are.

'It is a big deal I suppose but, the strange thing is that we don't feel that big, we really don't,' Nat ponders during a rare day off. 'We know that we're doing well here — and it's really great to make it in your own country, there's nothing like it — but because we're home so little we really don't get time to feel it.

'Things like that — meeting the president — well, you know, that's something special. But we've been home two weeks this year. We can't really measure our success.'

There have, obviously, been huge changes in the girls' lives since the release of their first single, none bigger perhaps than for Mel, who is, at time of press, an expectant mother, and Nicky, who is engaged to Robbie Williams. But at a grassroots level the girls are pretty much the same as they were the day they signed their London contract papers.

'We haven't changed as individuals, we are the same towards each other and around each other,' Shaznay reflects. 'I constantly look at the girls to notice if their attitudes or personalities have changed in some way and they haven't. We're the same as we ever were.'

Same as they ever were, perhaps ... except that now millions of music lovers, globally, know just what that means. Quite why they've struck a chord with international music fans is arguable, but Shaznay has her theories.

'We're not the best singers in the world. We're not Mariah Careys or Whitney Houstons but I think we all have unique voices. I think there are styles and different sounds in our voices and that's why they work so well together,' she says.

'And with the music we're not in one specific category, so people will never be able to judge our sound by what is going on around us or what other kind of music is doing well. You can't say what we do is hip-hop. Can't say it's pop. Can't say it's soul. It's not dance — so what is it?'

It's All Saints. It's unique. And thankfully there's more to come.

'We're back in the studio in August,' says Mel. 'We're dying to get back there because it's been so long. It'll be interesting to see what it brings because we've lived through different things since the first record. It'll be interesting to see how we've changed and how that affects the music.'

'All the stuff on the first album was when we were unknown,' Shaznay interjects. 'We were just a band that loved being in the studio and enjoyed the whole vibe of making tunes and striving to be known — not to be famous — to be known, more than just us four knowing our songs. Now we're in a band bigger than we ever thought. A band that's had a number-one single, two Brit awards, that's known all around the world. It will be interesting to see what we come up with.'

As somebody (at the Brits) once said: 'Nuff respect to anyone who gets up in the morning and knows what they want to do with their lives.' Because, surely, if they work hard enough at it, they will do well. And on that basis, All Saints will be having hits for a very — very — long time.

# NICKY

**Has All Saints turned out the way you expected it to?**
'I don't honestly think I've ever been happier in my life than I am right now. The group's very close, my family's happy and healthy and it seems to me that I'm in a very good position. It just seems to be getting better and better.

**What has been the highlight of it all for you?**
All these brilliant things have happened — the Brits, getting to number one and, for me, getting engaged. It's quite weird.

Getting engaged has made me so happy. It was very cool — we just arrived at the airport back from wherever and Rob was there, and it happened and we went home. That's it really. And then the next morning it was all over the papers — which just goes to show how quickly news spreads in this industry. That's one of the weirdest things now about being in All Saints. The press attention.

**When we first met you had just released 'I Know Where It's At' and you told me that you fancied Robbie Williams. Now you're engaged to him and the group is doing brilliantly. Don't you ever think 'woah, everything I wished for is coming true'?**
Er, no. Because, with the group, we've worked very hard to get to where we are right now. I've never worked so hard. I know that we're lucky. But we've also earned it.

# NATALIE

**You've had an amazing time.**
I know. When I think of all the things we've done and the times we've had, it's quite strange. I mean, the world music awards at Monaco was amazing — everything about it was great — the people, the food, meeting our heroes, like Puff Daddy. Astounding. The only thing that spoiled that trip was

meeting Mariah Carey. Monaco is a small country but her ego took up most of it!

**Any low points?**
For me, lack of sleep. A couple of months ago we were in Japan and I couldn't sleep. I knew I had all this work to do the next day and I was so, so tired. My body clock was all out and I didn't know what to do. I usually end up on the phone to my mum.

**Performing for the President of the United States must have been crazy.**
He was really cool actually. A really nice guy. He just hung out with us – I think he wanted to hang out more because it must have been boring with all those politicians. And he said he liked my boots. So he's cool.

**How do you see the future of the band now?**
I don't know. What scares me about all this is where we're going. I'm the only one in the band who doesn't sleep at night, worrying. In the beginning it was just us and we were doing our own thing. Now it's so much more of a business. We've got the next two years planned – for the tour and then targeting America – but after that I'm not sure.

**But you're happy?**
Oh yeah. We all are. We're all doing what we wanted to – performing, singing, writing. It *is* a dream come true.

# SHAZNAY

**No rest for the wicked then — you've already started on the new album.**
Yes. Well, I've got one song written and a few ideas for others. Whether they'll end up on the album or not, I'm not sure. But we are working on it, yeah.

**Is it hard to settle back into family life when you get home?**
Yeah. It's so hard to sit at the table and talk about the washing machine that's broken down with your mum. It's really hard to go back home and fit in. Everyday while we're away we're working so much we're surrounded by ten bodyguards, ten strangers who, if you say, 'I'm thirsty' will go and get you a drink. Then you come home and say, 'I'm thirsty' and your mum says, 'Get it yourself.'

**Do you think you'll cope with all of this?**
Yeah. We'll have to. The thing is to try and keep your head. I remember I was going out with a friend recently and we got ready and got to the door and I thought, 'How do we get there?' I'm used to having Johnny Buckland [All Saints' tour manager] there with the van or a car but my friend was saying, 'Get on the tube,' and I'm like, Nooo! I used to be a tubeaholic. I always had a travel card in my pocket. But the thought of using the tube freaked me out. I'm going to have to detach myself from that because one day in my life I will not have a Johnny Buckland with me. We got a cab that day in the end because I just couldn't get the tube to Oxford Street.

# MELANIE

**Has All Saints turned out the way you expected it to?**
Not exactly, no, because I don't think I ever had a full vision of what I expected it to turn out like. I didn't expect it to happen so fast or turn out on such a grand scale and I never expected it to be ... well, it's the work that I wasn't envisioning. We were happy just staying in London, never expected all this travel and promotion. We were content to be big in England, or London even or just being big in north London would have been fine with us! But it's crazy at the moment.

**Are you happy with what you've done musically?**
I think so. We still had to compromise to an extent though. Hopefully with the second album we won't have to so much, but as with anybody's first album you have to listen to your record company to some extent.

**How would you like to see All Saints progress?**
Wouldn't mind a couple of Grammys! And I think just to be left alone in the studio to get on with it – no interruptions and no interference and just to get on with it. That's what we want. Hopefully, by the time the book comes out, we'll have done quite a bit of it. It'll be great to be in the studio again.

And of course the tour is next year. We're rehearsing in March and April and then we're off. We're definitely looking forward to that. Definitely. It's what we've all been waiting for. Performing. It'll be great.